PROPOSED HIGH PERFORMANCE ORGANIZATION

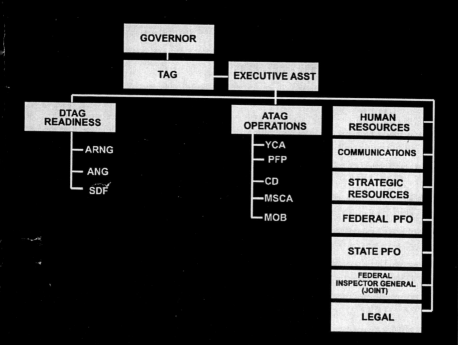

CURRENT STOVE PIPED ORGANIZATION

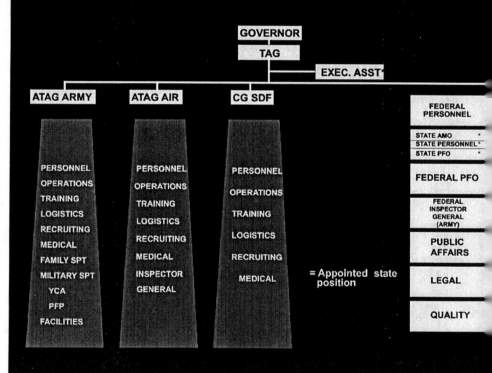

"A timely, straightforward approach to overcoming old-paradigm thinking. Provides food for thought, and growth, for all top-level executives."

Ron Barrett
V.P., Business & Organizational Development
International Beverage Management Corporation

• • • • • • • • •

"Sentell presents new management thought and a new management model to guide leaders of High Performance Organizations in the 1990s. Forceful, compelling, and persuasive!! *Fast, Focused, & Flexible* is one of the titles you must read in 1994."

H. Thomas Johnson
Portland State University
Author, *Relevance Regained*

• • • • • • • • •

"This is a valuable book that explains new concepts of future management systems. It is straightforward and easy to understand."

Luen Krisnakri
Governor, Petroleum Authority of Thailand

• • • • • • • • •

"*Fast, Focused, & Flexible* explores the fallacies of current management theory and leads to a clear understanding of what must be created. The concepts of process, leadership, systems, people, and an intense focus on customer needs are well developed and integrated into a compelling vision of the new organization."

J.A. Kelly
Director of Quality, Petrolite Corporation

• • • • • • • • •

"If you have five books to read this year, make *Fast, Focused, & Flexible* the first of them, reference it often, and start the change process now, especially if your business couldn't be better! Sentell has brilliantly integrated usually paradoxical disciplines into easily understandable language and has provided a highly useful foundation tool for people to lead the change process rather than be a victim to it."

John R. Wainwright
Sears Roebuck and Co. Executive (Retired)

• • • • • • • • •

"This book is about real implementation. To prosper in the '90s, you will have to be fast, focused, and flexible."

Robert Lorber, Ph.D.
Co-Author, *Putting the One-Minute Manager to Work*

"Very insightful! Clearly articulated! Right on target for managing at the speed of today's change. Integrates culture, process, strategy, and an overall customer mind-set."

Tim Mathewson
Manager, Work Process Improvement, Dow Chemical Co.

• • • • • • • • •

"Tennessee Associates has been working with our company for a long time. *Fast, Focused, & Flexible* embodies all our past successes and takes us another step into the future. An important book for the '90s and beyond."

Jim Terrill
CEO, Jefferson-Smurfit Corporation

• • • • • • • • •

"Refreshing to finally see someone put together a serious work that doesn't offer up a simplistic formula. Sentell clearly explains why and how a new 'from-the-ground-up' management system must be put in place."

Roger Slater
Author, *Integrated Process Management*
LTV Executive (Retired)

"A great book for the late '90s! *Fast, Focused, & Flexible* detects the most important business issues, and clearly and simply describes how to cope with them."

Federico Sada G.
Chairman of Anchor Glass Container Corporation
President of Vitro Envases Norteamerica

• • • • • • • • •

"A wealth of new thinking! *Fast, Focused, & Flexible* answers the fundamental questions that are at the heart of surviving and prospering in today's chaotic business world! Sentell tells it like it is! His writing follows his advice for leaders of High Performance Organizations: act swiftly, decisively, and with force, when required."

Bob Zollars
President, Baxter Healthcare Corporation
Hospital Supply/Scientific Products Division

• • • • • • • • •

"Clear presentation! Cuts through the conceptual jungle!"

Hans B. Thorelli, Ph. D.
Indiana University School of Business

FAST
FOCUSED
& FLEXIBLE

BOLD NEW IMPERATIVES
FOR THE
HIGH PERFORMANCE ORGANIZATION

Gerald D. Sentell

PRESSMARK INTERNATIONAL

Printing History
First Edition, 1994
    Second printing, 1994
    Third printing, 1995

Publisher's Cataloging in Publication
Sentell, Gerald D.
    Fast, focused & flexible : bold new imperatives for the high
performance organization / Gerald D. Sentell.
    p. cm.
    Includes bibliographic references and indexes.
    Preassigned LCCN: 94-65940
    1. Organizational change. 2. Organizational change--
Psychological aspects. I. Title. II. Title: Fast, focused and
flexible.

HD58.8.S458 1994   658.4'06
                                  QBI94-619

PRESSMARK INTERNATIONAL
◆ RESOURCES FOR IMPLEMENTATION ◆

Writing a book such as this is never an easy task. The unfairness is that the lives of the author's friends, colleagues, and family are often most affected during the process. Without their support, nothing could have been accomplished. So, I sincerely thank them all from the bottom of my heart.

A special tribute to my beautiful wife, Eade, who has shared the past quarter-century of my life. She is the patient and loving mother of our four high-performance children (Jerry, Gregg, Regina, and Gerina), the source of my strength and inspiration, and through it all, still my best friend.

ACKNOWLEDGMENTS

In order to achieve high performance, I was assisted in this book by several teams.

Members of the Senior Content Team who provided input to the ideas are senior officers of Tennessee Associates International:

Timothy Carpenter, my partner and Executive Vice President, Europe
Gerald Michaelson, Executive Vice President, Asia Pacific
Edward C. Miles, Vice President, U.S. Operations
Allen Pannell, President, U.S. Operations
Fred L. Smith, Chief Operating Officer

The Editorial Team, also members of the Tennessee Associates staff, worked diligently to "polish" the manuscript:

Gerald Michaelson, Team Leader
Sandy Belcher, for proofreading
Mark Carter-Piff, who provided valuable research
Marsha Cunningham, for her diligent work in layout and design
Susanne Dupes, who "translated" my writing into meaningful words
Connie Fancher, for publishing support
Priscilla Hall, our staff librarian, for her very valuable research
Lana Hickey, whose help with coordination was invaluable
Erny James, our talented staff artist who helped turn my ideas into
   pictures that led to improved ideas
Laurie Macnair, head of our Resource Center, for many important
   contributions
Karen Richardson, who thoroughly checked and double-checked the
   language structure
David Widener, who provided valuable research
and all my other colleagues at Tennessee Associates International

Recognition should go to James Cotham and Michael Raynor, who provided early editorial assistance; also, to James Neal and Daniel Newman for their work in reproducing and mailing countless drafts.

CONTENTS

The
High Performance
Organization

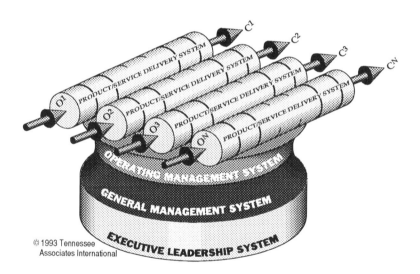

FOREWORD

It is refreshing to finally see a serious work that does more than offer a simplistic formula like so many of the management fads of the 1980s. For years, I have tried to tell anyone who would listen that "piecemeal problem solving" wouldn't cut it, and that a whole new system—from the ground up—had to be implemented.

I didn't have a good feel for the components of that system until I read *Fast, Focused & Flexible*. When I wrote *Integrated Process Management*, I used a six-step model to integrate many of the tools of the '80s. These tools were good, but none enabled us to see the whole picture. The first step in my model was "Creating the Positive Environment," which is largely what Dr. Sentell conveys in his book. I had no idea it was so all encompassing.

The concept of Endemic Overcapacity as explained in the book is fundamental to understanding how to be successful in any business. Another key concept is the idea that "general conditions require general solutions." In many respects, this is like trying to address special cause variation when common cause is the real culprit. How many times have we seen simplistic tools held up as solutions for companies whose management styles were "basket cases?"

Dr. Sentell is a brave warrior to give the term "paradigm" such a prominent place in this book, particularly in light of its overuse by those who don't understand what it really means. The concept of paradigms is absolutely essential to the overall content and is thoroughly explained here for the first time. The idea that the present system has to be totally scrapped can only be explained in terms of a paradigm shift.

The idea of asking what is *it* is long overdue. For example, the *it* (that we so sagely pronounce) has to start at the top. That is precisely the *it* that has to be scrapped and replaced by the new paradigm.

And, finally, someone has put to bed the "touchy, feely" aspect of corporate culture. Sentell clearly defines culture as a behavior rather than as a feeling.

I could go on and on, but I'll conclude by saying that this is the first time I have understood the differences between vision, mission, and guiding values. I suddenly discovered that I really did not understand them. But now, thanks to Sentell, I do!

There is no "quick fix." Sentell accomplishes what he set out to do, which is to provide the fundamental understanding that can help leaders make a difference.

Roger Slater
Author, *Integrated Process Management*
LTV Executive (Retired)

INTRODUCTION

Many organizations that were widely applauded for their success just a few years ago are in deep trouble today. The very concept and definition of organizational success, and the methodologies thought to deliver it, have become increasingly suspect. Paradoxically, today's success can be an excellent predictor of tomorrow's failure.

One fact beyond dispute is that global political, social, and economic conditions are changing at unprecedented rates. *Today, nothing is like it was; tomorrow, nothing will be like it is.* It should be very clear that traditional organizational structures and management practices are no longer adequate. They are obsolete!

What is less clear is exactly why traditional organizational structures and management methodologies are no longer effective and what specifically must be done to achieve high performance. Many people have written and lectured about "what to do." The prescriptive list is long and eclectic, with numerous mutually inconsistent approaches and ideas. For example, we find "experts" of various backgrounds and persuasions recommending that organizations should be excellent, become lean, develop "good" strategies, pursue quality awards, benchmark, plan everything carefully, or be spontaneous and "go with the flow." The list goes on and on. It should not be surprising that after much fanfare and early anecdotal support, these fads have failed to produce the promised results.

To succeed in tomorrow's dynamic and chaotic environment, organizations will have to change drastically. They must become simultaneously:

Fast—to seize new opportunities or respond instantaneously to unpredictable and dynamic changes in the marketplace.

Focused—to simultaneously optimize both customer satisfaction and organizational excellence.

Flexible—to accommodate significant, rapid, and unpredictable change without experiencing costly organizational trauma.

This book is for those who must plan and lead the change required to create High Performance Organizations. Numerous snapshots of unrelated cases and experiences will not suffice. This book will not offer partial solutions, sets of tools and techniques, or a series of vignettes and anecdotes. Instead, the focus will be on developing a clear, holistic understanding of both the "old" and "new" for leaders who must effect fundamental organizational transformation. This book will help leaders understand why current management concepts and practices are flawed and provide practical advice on planning and effecting the changes necessary to create a High Performance Organization—one that can accommodate new and critical performance imperatives.

Because executives are constantly under the pressure of time, they are more likely to read this book chapter-by-chapter than cover-to-cover in one session. Therefore, the chapters are designed to stand alone as well as to form an integral part of the whole.

- ♦ Chapter 1 describes the challenges facing organizations, along with the strategies and organizational implications required to cope with the new world order.
- ♦ Chapter 2 investigates the major inhibitors to the required fundamental organizational changes and points out that the biggest obstacle is the knowledge structures of those who must lead the change.
- ♦ Chapter 3 explains how "traditional" organizational models and management systems evolved and why they are now obsolete.
- ♦ Chapter 4 shows that the flaws in the traditional models and systems cannot be repaired and new ones must be developed.

- Chapter 5 addresses the profound changes required to replace these obsolete models and systems. The very "culture" of the organization must be re-created.
- Chapter 6 offers an overview of the fundamentally different organizational model required to meet the challenge of 21st-century markets and competition.
- Chapter 7 describes the leadership necessary for the successful implementation and operation of the new High Performance Organization.
- Chapter 8 reveals proven practical models to guide the planning and execution of these profound organizational changes.
- Conclusion provides brief discussions and insights about who ultimately must lead the changes necessary for any organization to survive and prosper into the next century.

Bold New Imperatives for the High Performance Organization

Develop an organization that will survive and prosper in the dynamic and chaotic future.

Design structures and systems to optimize strategies.

Design and lead organizations that are simultaneously:

> *Fast*—to seize new opportunities or respond instantaneously to unpredictable and dynamic changes in the marketplace.

> *Focused*—to simultaneously optimize both customer satisfaction and organizational excellence.

> *Flexible*—to accommodate significant, rapid, and unpredictable change without experiencing costly organizational trauma.

Search for new thinking.

Do not operate in the old paradigm simply because it is there.

Each of us is the source of his or her own misunderstandings.

Get "out of the box."

Create a radically different paradigm of management.

If you do what you've always done, you'll get what you've always gotten. If you only do it faster, you'll only get it quicker. If you change only words and not actions, you'll get "old wine in new bottles."

Management is a technology—the application of science and knowledge for practical purpose. Leaders must adopt appropriate management technologies; however, leadership transcends technology.

Changing management paradigms is much more difficult than changing logical, rational scientific paradigms.

Understand the new paradigm.

Understanding is not *I'll know it when I see it.*

Understanding is *I'll see it when I know it!*

Change behavior to create a different culture.

Training and education are catalysts of culture change.

Leaders must create the environment that nurtures the new culture.

Organizational culture is determined by relationships among dynamically interactive components.

Manage systems and processes, not people.

The structure is based on a hierarchy of process, not a hierarchy of power.

Shift the focus from output measures to processes and systems.

Recognize that high performance people are critical to the High Performance Organization.

It is a fundamental truth that people want to do well and be recognized for having done well.

People work best in teams where they are empowered to gather data and take action.

The quality of service is largely determined by the quality of the people providing the service.

Maintain a simultaneous focus on the customer and internal performance excellence.

Delighted customers are necessary. However, they alone do not ensure long-term prosperity.

World-class quality and productivity are necessary. They alone cannot create a High Performance Organization.

Variation is the enemy.

Chapter 1

The Challenge of the New Economic World Order

In chaos there is opportunity.

The magnitude and pace of change—social, economic, technological, political, and cultural—are increasing at a dramatic rate throughout the world. This rapid change creates chaotic times, and in chaos are the seeds of opportunities.

Consider the stream of news. The Soviet Union has imploded. The borders between East and West have disappeared. Differences continue, but overtly hostile blocs competing furiously for the hearts and minds of people are now a thing of the past. The effects of these global dynamics on many Western businesses and political leaders have been similar to responses encountered by adults experiencing their first earthquake.

I will never forget my first earthquake. The tremor was actually fairly insignificant. Since I had never experienced an earthquake, I immediately became anxious and felt a complete loss of control over my destiny. The steady earth beneath my feet had always been taken for granted. Every-

1

thing else might be potentially dangerous, but surely not the ground on which I stood—or so I thought.

On that memorable morning, the ground began its small and, thankfully, short-lived dance. My fear quickly became evident. This amused my California colleagues because their experiences with earthquakes enabled them to calmly accept what was happening. My anxiety was a result of my complete lack of comparable experience. I've encountered hurricanes and tornadoes far more dangerous and life-threatening, but this small earthquake threatened my most basic sense of security and well-being.

Many of today's leaders are encountering disturbing changes that leave them shaken, full of doubt, and wondering what to do. The magnitude of global change has battered organizations as their leaders try to react. Many continue to respond in the traditional manner—by doing what they have always done faster or by simply downsizing. But, as the old saying goes, "When we do what we have always done, we will get what we have always gotten." This is hardly an adequate method for coping with the magnitude of change facing us today and tomorrow.

Doing the same things faster only achieves the same results sooner. When a large, unsuccessful organization downsizes but does not make other fundamental changes, it just becomes a smaller, but still unsuccessful, organization.

The leaders of many organizations who failed to respond adequately have retired, been replaced, or have been subjugated to serious oversight by their boards of directors. New and different solutions are required. In order for organizations to succeed, the first step is to develop a better understanding of the rapidly changing environment in which they must struggle.

THE UNENDING QUAKE

Worldwide socioeconomic and political conditions have changed more profoundly during the last few years than at any time since the beginning of the Industrial Revolution. These unprecedented and unpredictable events are just the beginning of a new era of "earthquakes." Coping with change must now be the top priority of leaders throughout the world. A new dimension of change will affect all types of organizations.

General Electric Chief Executive Jack Welch said, "My view is that facing reality, in good times and in bad, is an ethical obligation for managers—indeed for anyone whose actions affect other people."[1]

The problem is that neither leaders nor their advisers seem to know how to cope with the reality of these continuing quakes. We need better ways to make predictions and better ways to respond to them. This is easy to say, but not easy to do (Figure 1.1).

The world is becoming less predictable. Five-year sales forecasts are no longer valid. The future of organizations is

3

A WORLD OF DOWNSIZING

Over Half of Europe's Big Firms Are Planning Work Force Cuts

Downsizing in Next 2 Years Is Expected to Surpass Rate of Moves in U.S.

Dofasco Will Lay Off 10% of Its Employees And Cut Production

HAMILTON, Ontario

Eli Lilly to Cut 4,000 Salaried Contract Jobs

Deutsche Aerospace Says Work Force Cuts To Total 20% by 1996

MUNICH, G—

Peugeot Citroen To Cut 5,000 Jobs, Union Leaders Say

PARIS, France

Apple Planning To Lay Off 16% Of Work Force

VW Says It Has 30,000 Workers It Doesn't Need

WOLFSBURG, German

Nissan May Eliminate Another 1,000 Jobs; Sales For— Dims

Woolworth To Shutter 10% Of Its Stores

Plans to Eliminate 13,000 Jobs

GE Will Revamp Jet Engine Unit, Cutting 1,500 Jobs

Michelin's North America Unit Slates Layoffs of 2,500, or 9% of Work Force

Alcoa Will Cut 25 ~~ of U.S. Capacity, Lay Off 2% of Its Domestic Work F—

IBM Posts $8.04 Billion 2nd-Period Loss, — Dividend, Plans 35,000 Job Cuts

Ameritech Corp. Management Layoffs to Cut Between 1,200 and 1,500 Jobs

—rcedes to Cut —rman Force —y 14,000 Jobs

Figure 1.1

CHANGES IN THE ECONOMIC WORLD ORDER

THE HORIZONTAL CORPORATION

Hierarchy is dying. In the new corporate model, you manage across–not up and down.

As Discounting Rises In Japan, People Learn To Hunt for Bargains

THE CONTINEN... WAKE-UP CALL

WELCOME to the REVOLUTION

...partment Stores, Shops Are Hurt, S. Firms...

Japan, Economically And Politically Ailing, Is Sinking Into Gloom

Euphoria of '80s Boom Ends As People Cut Spending Amid Worries Over Jobs

Emboldened by Strong Economy, China Speaks Out and Commands Respect

EC Approves $7.66 Billion Aid Package In Bid to Revive Sluggish Steel Industry

Spanish Banks, Hurting From Bad Debt, Interest Rates, See 1994 Profi...

Next year "is going to be difficult"

IS GERMANY REUNIFICATION FAILING?

U.S. Surpasses Japan As Leading Producer Of Semiconductors

The U.S. for the first time in sev... surpassed Japan

MANAGING IN THE ERA OF CHANGE

Foreign Executives Sing GATT's Praises, But Few Anticipate Immediate Benefits

"It's the best Christmas present for the world econo..."

Trade Pact Is Set by 117 Nations, Slashing Tariffs, Sub...

World Trade Accord Finally W... Up By 117 Countries

British Steel's Great Pain Turns to Profit

Despite Woes, Other EC Steelmakers Resist Cutbacks

MIRACLE CURES BE IN YOUR CEL...

In Global Vacuum, Tyranny Advances

Those willing to use brute force on behalf of absolute power have a green light.

Figure 1.1 (cont.)

5

inherently nonlinear and cannot be explained with linear mathematical models. The future can be better explained using the "mathematics of chaos."

On Chaos

In his intriguing best-seller, *Jurassic Park,* author Michael Crichton relates a practical and understandable discussion of "chaos theory" through the words of mathematician Ian Malcolm. Citing several examples of nonlinear dynamics, Malcolm says that the island amusement park won't work.

"Pool balls. You hit a pool ball, and it starts to carom off the sides of the table...Since you know the force of the ball, and the mass of the ball, and you can calculate the angles at which it will strike the walls, you can predict the future behavior of the ball...It turns out you can't predict more than a few seconds into the future. Because almost immediately very small effects—imperfections in the surface of the ball, tiny indentations in the wood of the table—start to make a difference. So it turns out that this simple system of a pool ball on a table has an unpredictable behavior."[2]

Later in the book, the mathematician ties fractal geometry to chaos theory to further justify his conclusions: "...fractal geometry appears to describe real objects in the natural world...a sameness from the smallest to the largest and this sameness of scale also occurs for events...You see, the fractal idea of sameness carries within it an aspect of recursion, of doubling back on itself, which means that events are unpredictable...Chaos theory teaches us that straight linearity...simply does not exist...Life is actually a series of encounters in which one event may change those that follow in a wholly unpredictable, even devastating way."[3]

The seven iterations of events that Crichton uses to show the underlying implications of chaos theory are:[4]

1. "At the earliest drawings of the fractal curve, few clues to the underlying mathematical structure will be seen."
2. "With subsequent drawings of the fractal curve, sudden changes may appear."
3. "Details emerge more clearly as the fractal curve is redrawn."
4. "Inevitably, underlying instabilities begin to appear."
5. "Flaws in the system will now become severe."
6. "System recovery may prove impossible."
7. "Increasingly, the mathematics will demand the courage to face its implications."

This same series of events expressed in these iterations can be applied to the chaos facing organizations. To survive, we must understand the implications of the underlying order. As a profound summary of this thought, Malcolm adds these words of wisdom: "That's a deep truth about the structure of our universe. But, for some reason, we insist on behaving as if it were not true."[5]

COPING WITH THE CHALLENGE OF CHAOS

Over the years, a few adages have proven extremely helpful when I have needed to sort out life's normal everyday complexities in pursuit of explanations. One of the most universal and valuable of these has been:

General conditions require general solutions; special conditions require special solutions.

This simple theorem is very useful, but difficult to apply correctly. Both the power of the theorem and difficulty of application become clearer when we understand how to distinguish general conditions from special conditions.

General conditions include fundamental socioeconomic changes. For example, the steel industry is confronted with a worldwide glut of capacity. At the same time, the steel markets are dwindling due to the substitution of lighter or different materials for steel. If a steel mill responds to these general conditions as special conditions of limited duration, rather than general, long-term problems, the results are unlikely to be successful. The global organizational responses required to cope with general conditions are significantly different from the unique organizational responses required to cope with special conditions.

The new economic world order reflects chaos in the technical sense of chaos theory—a general condition that affects everyone and every organization to some degree. Any effort to cope with these conditions must be general rather than special if organizations are to survive and prosper. One of the most profound changes affecting industries and organizations throughout the world manifests itself in new and startlingly different competitive conditions and market structures. The term I have coined to identify these new and different competitive conditions and market structures is *Endemic Overcapacity*:

> *Overcapacity* simply means there is more supply than demand at price levels that permit acceptable operating margins.
>
> *Endemic,* in this context, means that the threat of overcapacity faces every organization—if not today, then in the very near future.

Just as we say that a disease is endemic in a particular area, we say that overcapacity can be endemic to all markets—particularly global markets. For example, if I travel to a country in which hepatitis is endemic, it is not certain that I will become a victim of the disease. However, if I stay long enough, there is a very high probability that I will eventually become ill with hepatitis, even if I take the proper precautions.

Similarly, in business, no matter how unique I believe my products and services to be, my organization will be exposed to Endemic Overcapacity. Even if I take precautions, I will probably suffer pressures from price competition, reduced margins, and downsizing.

Endemic Overcapacity occurs when products and services are continuously subject to competitive market conditions, causing their rapid transformation into commodities. A commodity is a product or service in which the market—not the producer—sets the prices. As a result, operating margins can be controlled only through cost containment.

ENDEMIC OVERCAPACITY

The alarming turmoil in general conditions has several fundamental, underlying dimensions:

First, *technology*, the practical application of science and knowledge, *is undergoing its own revolution*. New ways are being created to do old things, meet old needs, do new things, and meet new needs. The pace of technological change is spreading throughout the world at a breathtaking rate. Newly developing economies and industries are applying new technologies more rapidly than ever before.

Second is *the pace of change that is related to the spread of technology*. In the past, organizations could plan product life cycles of years. Now months—or sometimes weeks—

are all that can be expected. Plants and equipment become obsolete with astonishing speed; markets are gained and lost overnight.

The third underlying dimension is *the globalization of the economy*—racing ahead with more impact than predicted by any forecast. The new world order has accelerated the speed of change. Any market that provides relatively high margins and returns will be bombarded by competition from around the world. Any process or equipment will eventually be under pressure from newer processes and equipment produced in countries not recognized as competitors today. Both competition and market opportunities are springing up at an unprecedented pace in Asia, the former Eastern bloc, South America, and Africa.

Finally, *customers are becoming increasingly sophisticated* and aware of the opportunities presented by the new competitive world order. Customers expect high value and innovations in products, services, and processes.

These dimensions reduce the time that successful products or services will be able to maintain margin and share. The result is the new general condition of Endemic Overcapacity, which eventually affects most organizations.

COPING WITH ENDEMIC OVERCAPACITY

Given the general condition of Endemic Overcapacity, we need a strategy—a general solution.

Most business is in the realm of commodities, where the market sets the price, rather than products, where the organization sets the price (within reason). The term "product" includes the <u>intangible benefits</u> that result from <u>tangible things</u>. Everything we purchase is a product and may or may not come with associated services.

When products are new and scarce, gross margins on sales can be relatively high. But over time, margins are squeezed down to lower commodity ranges of less than 7%. In the commodity business, the way to survive is to maintain expected levels of quality and service performance, while steadily reducing costs.

Another way to maintain margins is to provide value-added services that can yield higher margins. For example, Lexus is famous for its after-sale service. Because customers are willing to pay more for enhanced benefits, a higher margin can be obtained.

However, Endemic Overcapacity means that competitors will soon duplicate extra-value services and high-value products, and will drive margins down. They become commodities when the market sets the price (Figure 1.2). The new commodity performance level becomes the new minimum standard expected by customers.

As Endemic Overcapacity extends its reach and intensity, less time is required for extra-value products and services to devalue into commodities. To survive and pros-

COPING WITH ENDEMIC OVERCAPACITY
– A General Solution for a General Condition

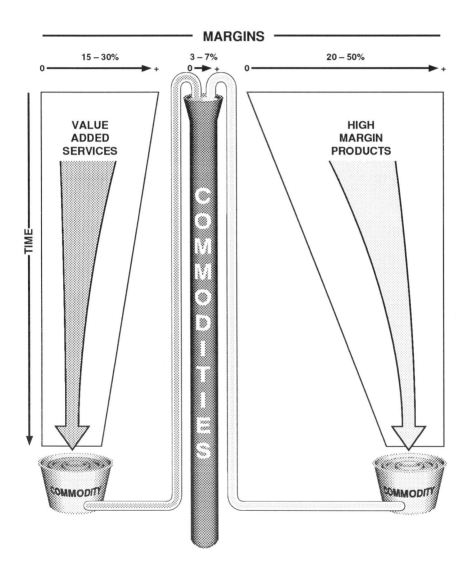

Figure 1.2

13

per, an organization must steadily develop new high-margin, value-added products and services, while continuing to reduce costs and improve services in the commodity lines. This simple concept is difficult to execute.

Strategy Dictates Structure

To successfully implement the strategies necessary to cope with Endemic Overcapacity, organizations must be structured so they are simultaneously fast, focused, and flexible.

The structure of an organization must follow its strategy. Too many managers try to fit strategy to structure and cannot understand why performance is lacking. Or, even worse, the organization is restructured without first establishing the correct strategy and designing a structure through which it can be effectively implemented (Figure 1.3).

The strategies must be flexible enough to cope with the significant, never-ending changes encountered in the world of Endemic Overcapacity. The organization must be able to respond rapidly and smoothly while remaining focused on both the customer and its own performance. Organizations can no longer restructure to handle each new crisis. Prosperity and survival are at stake.

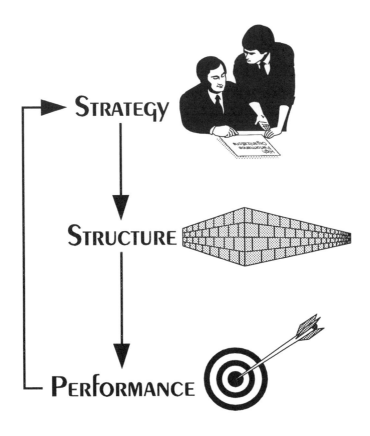

Figure 1.3

To attain performance objectives,
strategy and structure must be aligned.

CHAPTER 2

THE INTERACTION OF PARADIGMS AND KNOWLEDGE STRUCTURES

We don't see things as they are, we see them as we are.
—Anais Nin

Paradigms enable problem solving and decision making to occur in a familiar, understandable framework until they are made obsolete by a more accurate model. New paradigms are devised as better ways to explain a complex reality.

Truth is viewed through each individual's perceptual framework. As our experiences increase, our picture of truth changes, but truth itself remains constant. It is our understanding and perception of truth that can change.

For example, when Copernicus and Galileo suggested that the Earth rotated around the Sun, rather than that all heavenly bodies traveled around the Earth, they had not changed reality at all. Instead, they offered a new model of how the universe functioned, and their supporting explanation (or paradigm) provided a better understanding of reality. The new paradigm replaced the existing geocentric paradigm and made it obsolete (Figure 2.1). This change did not

THE GEOCENTRIC MODEL

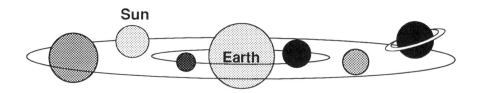

THE COPERNICAN MODEL

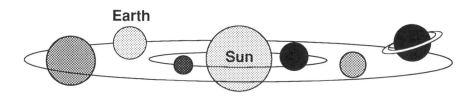

Figure 2.1

transpire instantaneously, nor did it happen without pain and cost.

Many of today's general conditions are paradigmatic in origin. The traditional management paradigm no longer effectively predicts these conditions. Those who continue to follow the current organizational paradigm encounter increasing difficulties. Many organizations have already failed; others fail daily. Therefore, a new paradigm is needed.

WHAT PARADIGMS ARE NOT

A paradigm is much more than just a way of doing things, or a given mindset, or a preconceived notion. As the notion of paradigms has gained popularity, the tendency has been to identify many changes as new paradigms.

The concept of paradigms has been trivialized by its oversimplification and, in many ways, has come to be little more than a cliché. This trivialization has led to the widespread and mistaken assumption that each of us has his or her own paradigms. However, a paradigm is independent of any individual's perceptual or cognitive processes. In other words, each person cannot and does not have a personal paradigm because paradigms are external. Each of us has "knowledge structures" that determine how we think, but these structures are not paradigms. In fact, these individual knowledge structures may inhibit our ability to recognize or accept a new paradigm.

At least two types of knowledge structures are relevant: cognitive psychologists have labeled these as schema and analogy.[1]

♦ A *schema* is abstract and generic. For example, we believe that people in a certain business behave in a certain way. Schemata (plural) are the fundamental elements upon which all information processing depends.

♦ An *analogy* is specific and concrete. For example, we remember when we were hired or when we lost a sale. One way we make sense of new situations is by using an analogy to compare new situations to old situations.

Unlike paradigms, schemata and analogies are clearly unique to each individual and are stored in our long-term memory. They interact to provide insight and guidance, especially when we encounter significant change. When schemata and analogies reinforce one another, new information is readily accepted. However, when new information does not mesh with our personal schemata or repertory of analogies, it receives little consideration or may be completely ignored.

THE DIFFICULTY OF PARADIGM CHANGE

Labeling every habitual action, deeply held belief, or current practice a paradigm dangerously inflates the word. A paradigm shift is not just a new idea or innovation. It is a complete restructuring of systems of thought based on a central fundamental premise. To claim that procedural changes are a genuine paradigm shift is to mistake a part for the whole.

In almost every genuine paradigm shift, it has taken a relatively long time for the new paradigm to be accepted.

This is true no matter how powerful or useful a new paradigm might be. The question is "why?"

New paradigms are not derived from the steady progress of knowledge within old paradigms because research in any particular field is conducted within the scope of the existing paradigm. Instead, new paradigms are the result of radically different approaches to problems the old paradigm could not explain.

Understanding a new paradigm requires a new way of thinking—and an awareness that a new paradigm is necessary. Discovering and understanding the new paradigm is not a case of "I'll know it when I see it," but:

"I'll see it when I know it."

There is an ongoing struggle to really understand the nature of that all-elusive *it*. We see what we believe is true. When people are presented with information contrary to their internal knowledge, they often do not understand *it*. So, *knowing it* makes it easier to *see it*.

It has often been said that "I may not be able to tell you what quality is, but I know quality when I see it." That may be an acceptable statement for a customer to make, but it hardly suffices for a provider of goods or services. An "I'll know it when I see it" mentality keeps us looking for the unknown. In contrast, "I'll see it when I know it" indicates a sound understanding of what "it" is.

Significant progress results only from the theory-shattering changes of a paradigm shift. We resist paradigm shifts because they alter our most basic assumptions about the world around us.

The ability to accept a new paradigm is not a function of individual intelligence. We all know highly intelligent executives who continue to manage in a style based on old paradigms. In fact, the most intelligent people often have difficulty accepting paradigm shifts. Too often, institutions of higher learning have perpetuated the old paradigm. For example, years after many organizations fully embraced and practiced the principles of quality, a college course on quality could not be found. One major university professor declared that quality was "too deceptively simple" to teach at an institution of higher learning.

MAKING THE SHIFT

Making a paradigm shift can be enormously difficult for a variety of reasons. Typically, the best tactic to facilitate paradigm change is to encourage managers to be alert to the need to adopt a new paradigm. However, there is little information available to help managers understand and cope with the changes necessary to plan and lead a paradigm shift in their organization.

Most attempts to implement new paradigm systems have been less successful than expected. Regardless of how enthusiastically changes are embraced, expect only partial success, and possibly failure, unless there are radical shifts in the concepts that drive management and upon which the organization is structured. Theory and effective practices are more closely linked than most people realize. It is almost impossible to successfully implement and sustain significantly different practices without the supporting conceptual foundations.

PERSONAL BARRIERS TO UNDERSTANDING

Cognitive theory defines two aspects of information processing supportive of my experience and research with organizations and their leaders:

+ Schematic information processing occurs "top-down"—in other words, from the whole to the part. The significance of top-down processing is that we ignore or trivialize information that does not fit our personal knowledge structures. We are more sensitive to information that is consistent with what we already know.

+ Our insight into one area is often obtained from another seemingly similar area. For instance, the term "historical analogy" implies that if two or more events separated in time agree in one respect, then they may also agree in another. For example, consider Henry Cabot Lodge's use of the Munich analogy in justifying U.S. intervention in Vietnam:[2]

+ Appeasement in Munich occurred as a result of Western indolence.
+ Appeasement in Vietnam was also occurring as a result of Western indolence.
+ Appeasement in Munich resulted in a world war.
+ Therefore, appeasement in Vietnam would also result in a world war.

The misuse of historical analogies plaguing government policy makers similarly affects commercial decision makers. Consider this typical recession analogy:

+ Past recessions have been of a cyclical nature and of relatively short durations (a few quarters at most).
+ Current economic conditions reflect patterns similar to past recessions.
+ Recessions have always been replaced by a cyclical rebound in which sales volumes and prices move sharply upward.
+ Therefore, if we patiently conduct business as usual, the upturn in the economy will do much to resolve problems.

Prior to understanding recent information on the practical applications of cognitive psychology, I struggled with a similar problem—how to help managers become more effective in multi-cultural, multi-national environments. The greatest obstacle was not the lack of information, education, or good intentions. On the contrary, there was generally <u>too much</u> information. Highly educated, sensitive managers continued to blunder even though their preparation was very thorough.

My research revealed that individual managers almost always process new information using historical analogies based on what they already know or believe they know. I call this problem "meocentrism" (me-centered). In other words, when trying to understand and cope with events, individuals are their own source of problems. Pogo was correct when he said, "We have met the enemy and it is **us.**"

A typical example of meocentrism is the entrepreneur whose corporate headquarters was filled with portraits of himself. He complained that "you just can't get good people." When voted out by his own board of directors, he left the company protesting that everyone else was wrong.

Experiences that are *culture-centered, time-centered,* and *location-centered* form an individual's cognitive schemata—meocentrism. These three facets are interactive.

The *culture-centered* facet is derived from an individual's basic psychological programming. It is learned through social, educational, and other related experiences. Individuals from the same kind of educational and family backgrounds are likely to have more similar cognitive structures than people from widely diverse backgrounds.

The *time-centered* facet interacts with major generational influences to profoundly affect an individual's cognitive map. The schemata of a given generation are very much a function of time and events. For example, a Baby Boomer would have a distinctively different perspective on politics and war than a person who was born during the Great Depression.

The *location-centered* facet simply implies where experiences were gained by individuals when profound generational events occurred. For example, people who served in the Vietnam War interpret similar events differently from those who did not.

The ability to recognize when an old paradigm needs to be replaced with a new one requires a clear understanding of the new paradigm. We must make a conscious effort to ensure that our existing knowledge structures do not cause us to ignore or misinterpret information. Often those who claim to be open-minded are actually highly prejudiced; they see what they think they know. Objectivity is not natural; it must be sought and nurtured.

TRADITIONAL DATA
DOES NOT PROVE PARADIGMS

Since paradigms are frameworks for understanding data, it should come as no surprise that data is never, in and of itself, the instrument of change. Any observations can be included in the existing paradigm framework and therefore considered to be the truth. By itself, no single observation can ever disprove a paradigm. Because people verify their observations based on their belief in the old paradigm, the proof they need before they will change is often impossible to attain. This is a classic Catch-22.

The only way to resolve this issue is to demand predictions of a paradigm. Then there is no question concerning validity—either the predictions come true or they don't. Choosing a new management paradigm involves an extremely complex set of issues. Predictions can be made, but it may be years (or decades) before we can determine viability. In a world characterized by Endemic Overcapacity, this wait-and-see attitude is a luxury few can afford. Consequently, we are forced to choose a management paradigm based on other criteria.

It is not enough to believe that the current paradigm is fundamentally flawed; we must understand why it is flawed. We then need a clear picture of an operable new paradigm that enables us to successfully lead our organization through the changes associated with a paradigm shift.

FROM MEANINGFUL CONCEPT TO EMPTY CLICHÉ

Modern life seems to be subject to an almost continuous barrage of fads. New fads enjoy a period of intense interest and popularity. Then they become overused and fade into the realm of the cliché—or are forgotten.

Many important management concepts and philosophies have been destroyed through overuse—for example, management by objectives and quality circles. The search then starts for a new, exciting, and unproven concept to

From Concept to Cliché
Value Over Time

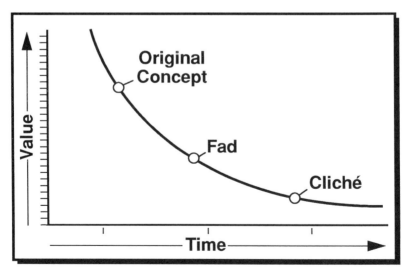

Figure 2.2

repeat the cycle. The value curve of a concept falls over time until it eventually approaches zero value (Figure 2.2).

The original concept of paradigm is one of the most important concepts to appear in the last several decades. It began in the realm of science and passed through the social sciences into management, where it has proven to be of great value. The inevitable overuse has caused this powerful paradigm concept to become confused with individual perceptions and knowledge structures. Its very success has led to its devaluation.

When the need for a concept continues to exist, but the original term has been devalued, a new term is introduced and the entire process repeats itself.

In this book, I try to swim against the tide. Important and valuable concepts such as paradigm and culture are used with careful and precise definitions. All of us are subject to the limitations imposed by our knowledge structures, so consider the definitions carefully. Otherwise, the power of the ideas can be lost through definitional differences.

CHAPTER 3

THE EVOLUTION OF THE TRADITIONAL MANAGEMENT PARADIGM

Truth is a phantom never showing itself for a moment except to ceaselessly flee.

– Henri Poincaré

Organizations evolve continuously from the day they are formed, and those that do not adapt soon fail. This ongoing environmental change has been referred to as Social Darwinism—the survival of the fittest. Some people take exception to the views surrounding Darwin's theory of evolution, but most would agree that competition among organizations amounts to a life-and-death struggle. Typically, barring outside influence, those who survive are the fittest.

Organizational development involves the study of the forces that differentiate survivors from failures. Those organizational behavior patterns that lead to apparent success or failure become the ones that other organizations strive to emulate or avoid. To remain effective, leaders must understand the real causes for their success. If they do not, any risk is too great because either success or failure will destroy the organization.

Generally speaking, there are two fundamental methodologies for changing organizations. The first involves relatively small changes within the parameters and boundaries of the existing paradigm. The second requires major changes necessitated when replacing one paradigm with another. The first is not a paradigm shift; the second one is. By definition, paradigm shifts are not daily occurrences—they are infrequent and profound.

ORGANIZATIONS BEFORE THE INDUSTRIAL REVOLUTION

The foundations of the current management paradigm were laid in Western Europe during the Industrial Revolution. Prior to this, the production system involved highly skilled artisans and craftsmen working alone or in very small groups to transform inputs into finished, marketable products. This type of production system generated low volumes of high quality outputs at high cost—the opposite of the mass-production paradigm.

In this system, the master craftsman was personally involved with the entire production process from the selection and purchase of inputs to the delivery of final outputs. The master's eye ensured that high quality was attained without waste as he tried to optimize the conversion of raw materials into a finished product.

At the dawn of the Industrial Revolution, new forces unleashed significant social and economic changes. Many of the craftsmen and skilled production workers were victims of the plague that ravaged Western Europe. New power elites replaced the old, feudalism died, and science and knowledge were rediscovered. By today's standards, those changes were painfully slow, but by the standards of the medieval period, they were lightning swift.

Chaos theory should help us understand that those changes led to unexpected and unpredictable outcomes. A broad range of events and conditions combined to facilitate the Industrial Revolution that eventually led to the birth of the mass-production paradigm.

THE EVOLUTION OF THE TRADITIONAL MANAGEMENT PARADIGM

New technologies permitted the substitution of more readily available semiskilled laborers for the highly skilled craftsmen, who required long training periods. As a result, per unit production costs began a steady and often precipitous decline.

In the craftsman era, there was an implicit global optimum because one person oversaw the entire process. With the introduction of specialization, each process was separated into subprocesses and each person specialized in one subprocess. The fundamental concept upon which specialization is based is that if each step is optimized, the global optimum will be achieved when the component steps are combined. This is based on the assumption that the sum of the local optima is equal to the global optimum. So, if mold making is optimized, polishing is optimized, etc., the final product should be an optimum output (Figure 3.1).

LOCAL OPTIMIZATION

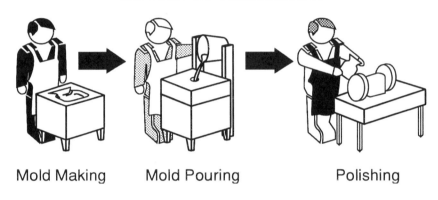

Mold Making   Mold Pouring   Polishing

Figure 3.1

This logic is intuitively appealing. When people look at the principle of specialization in concept or see it in practice, they have a tendency to think its value is obvious. Regardless of its appeal, striving for individual local optimization will not achieve the global optimum. The consequences of local optimization are waste, poor quality, and dissatisfied customers.

If we arbitrarily separate any generic process into a set of subprocesses (Figure 3.2), we can then see that each process

A PROCESS

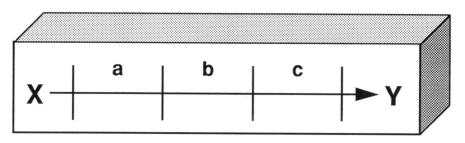

Figure 3.2

is dependent upon the other. The sum of the local optima is equal to the global optimum <u>only</u> when all the segments are independent of one another. However, this is not the situation in the overwhelming majority of organizational processes. It is at this point that the practical implications of chaos theory first became obviously relevant. *Prior to this stage of the evolution of the traditional paradigm, few clues to the flaws would have been seen.* As time passed and organizations grew, the flaws became all too apparent.

The Traditional Management Paradigm

The fundamental concept of specialization became one of the foundations upon which organizations were built. Specialization became the heart and soul of the traditional management paradigm.

Early industrialists were obsessed with seeking new technologies and methods to increase production. The need for additional output bred increased automation. Wherever machines could replace human effort, output increased. The increased productivity outweighed the cost of automation, and profits increased.

Automation and specialization combined to encourage further segmentation of work flow. In automated factories, production was simplified into a series of steps. More steps meant simpler and better opportunities for increased automation (Figure 3.3).

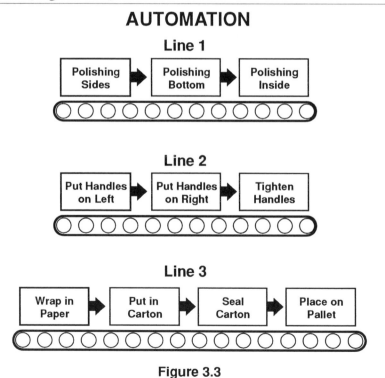

Figure 3.3

Increases in technology moved the production process further from the customer. Fewer people had contact with or an interest in the ultimate customer. According to chaos theory: *it is at this stage of evolution of the traditional paradigm of management that organizations began to encounter sudden and unexpected change.* In other words, the clues to the flaws inherent in the structure underlying the traditional management paradigm began to manifest themselves.

A central outgrowth of the traditional management paradigm is suboptimization. The real need is to optimize the total value chain from origination through consumption (Figure 3.4).

During the Industrial Revolution, organizations grew in the rapidly expanding economies and became highly functionalized. The process flow from input to output was no longer separated into simpler sequential tasks but instead into various functional departments from purchasing through sales and distribution. The implications of suboptimization remain unchanged regardless of the size of the components. The overall performance of the organization cannot be optimized by individually optimizing the performance of each component.

Many organizations simultaneously produce a wide variety of products and services. Traditional organizations manage an endless succession of departmental activities—down columns—instead of managing the process flow from

THE VALUE CHAIN

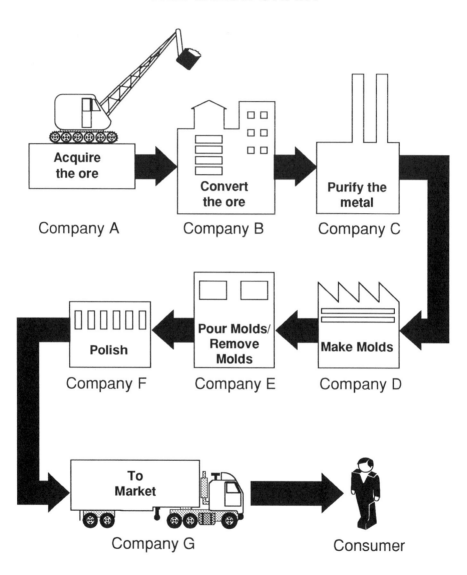

Figure 3.4

input to consumption—across a row (Figure 3.5). Where departmental activities involve many product lines, it is difficult to measure and evaluate organizational performance. The larger the organization, the more difficult it is to achieve accurate cross-functional measures.

A MULTI-PRODUCT/SERVICE ORGANIZATION

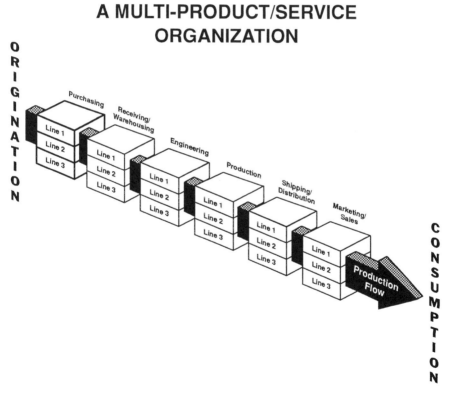

Figure 3.5

39

As organizations became more complex, the need for information to guide management increased dramatically. One might say that apples, oranges, peaches, and pears were compared as equals. Quite understandably, the performance measures that evolved were based on costs and other financial indexes. Performance was judged on the basis of simplistic financial correlates that were already biased by the effects of local optimization.

Consider the case we encountered in one organization in the food industry. Demand throughout the year was fairly constant on most items, and the overall goal was a consistent flow of shipments to retailers. However, to optimize sales and marketing, quarterly sales bonuses were established. At the end of each quarter, price concessions encouraged retailers to buy in large quantities and keep inventory in their warehouses. Since retailers placed huge orders, the salespeople received large bonuses, and quarterly quotas were achieved.

However, manufacturing, packaging, and shipping operations were suboptimized by the growth spurts at the end of each quarter. Resulting inefficiencies affected margins and the performance of the entire organization suffered. In effect, local optimization changed a linear demand into a wildly fluctuating demand that compromised the company's profitability and quality. As chaos theory states: *this is the point where details emerge more clearly and the inevitable underlying instabilities begin to appear. The early, unusual patterns begin to repeat themselves and grow in intensity.*

Many managers emphasize achieving results each quarter, and place great emphasis on the fourth quarter because this determines results for the year. Unfortunately, optimizing quarters will not optimize the year, and optimizing years will not optimize the decade because the years and their component quarters are interdependent (Figure 3.6).

PROBLEMS OF OPTIMIZATION

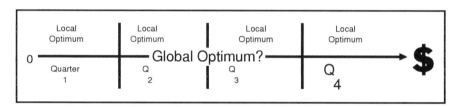

Figure 3.6

Just as in the case of the food company, special efforts to optimize the performance of one quarter can produce less than optimized results in subsequent quarters as well as in the performance of the organization as a whole. Even when financial measures are both accurate and appropriate, they are not necessarily very good management tools. Financial results are often little more than composite measures of an organization's efficiency or size. The pitfalls and weaknesses associated with these measures are well documented in *Relevance Regained*, by Professor H. Thomas Johnson:

"Impeding the revolutionary changes companies must make to be totally customer driven is management information. Specifically, the performance measures most companies use to control behavior encourage employees to subordinate customer satisfaction to accounting results. Accounting-based performance measures drive employees to manipulate processes and cajole customers in order to achieve cost and revenue targets. Inevitably, this practice diminishes competitiveness and impairs long-run profitability."[1]

THE INTERACTION OF ORGANIZATIONS ALONG THE VALUE CHAIN

Relatively few organizations control the entire production process from origin until the goods or services are received by the ultimate customer. The production process often involves several different organizations. Numerous vendors supply the components for an automobile or appliance; similarly, a financial institution or hospital uses a variety of outside resources. Each of these suppliers, in turn, would have other suppliers.

For example, a hospital might depend on a variety of resources. Supplies and medicines would come from producers through distributors to the hospitals, and outside physicians and doctors would provide medical services.

A variety of different products and services ranging from surgery to outpatient care are provided to distinctly different customers (Figure 3.7).

LINKAGE IN A VALUE CHAIN
(Healthcare Example)

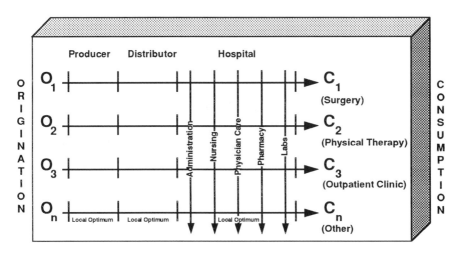

Figure 3.7

The linked organizations and departments through which inputs are transformed into outputs of goods or services is called a "value chain." This is where real value is added.

The craft-based enterprise handled the complete value chain from origin to consumption. Today's complex organizations rely on specialization and automation, which leads to suboptimization, which in turn leads to waste and misallocation of resources. The inefficiency of the modern

43

value chain is a general condition resulting from the traditional paradigm and not a special condition resulting from economic conditions, foreign competition, or poor management. Chaos theory explains: *this is where flaws in the system become severe.*

One example of a general condition inherent in the traditional paradigm is inadequate or poor organizational communications—both internal and external. An example of poor external communications is antagonistic vendor-supplier relationships that seriously disrupt the value chain. Internal communication problems include departmental turf battles consuming energy that would be better spent on meeting the customer's requirements. These communication problems are general conditions that require general paradigmatic solutions.

STRUCTURE OF THE TRADITIONAL PARADIGM

In growing enterprises, there was clearly a need for some type of organizational structure. Managers did not see a need to integrate the complex flow from production through distribution as much as they saw the need to coordinate ever-increasing numbers of organizational "chunks."

For an answer, pioneer industrialists looked, logically enough, at organizations that coordinated the activities of large numbers of people—the church, the government, and the army—all of which were rigid hierarchies. In fact, the very concept of organization carried with it the notion of a rigid hierarchy. The view was that anything that lacked hierarchy also lacked order. Industry adopted the traditional hierarchical management model by default.

The traditional hierarchical structure has led to overspecialization throughout the organization. For example, engineers specialize in certain areas of design and are promoted in that particular specialty. If successful, they may eventually rise to the level of chief product engineer, where they must resolve the conflicting goals of other similarly tunnel-visioned specialists. The specialization that hierarchy demands precludes a holistic approach and encourages suboptimization. It also spawns autocratic cultures that emphasize controlling, directing, and reporting on activities and outputs rather than guiding and coaching people.

Many who extol the virtues of traditional hierarchical management admit that "as practiced presently, hierarchy undeniably has its drawbacks—there is a widespread view that [it] kills initiative, crushes creativity, and has therefore seen its day."[2] Proponents of traditional hierarchical management systems believe that its problems are the result of misunderstandings of the theory and mistakes in correct implementation. The argument is that if we had understood "it," "it" would have worked.

The problems associated with traditional hierarchy, such as lack of creativity, interdepartmental rivalry, and suboptimization, are inevitable. No amount of understanding or finesse in implementation will overcome the unfortunate consequences of a traditional hierarchy. Chaos theory warns that: *the flaws are so severe that they may make system recovery impossible. Increasingly, the implications will demand that leaders have the courage to face the facts.*

One of the fundamental problems with traditional hierarchy lies in the structural relationship between people and the personal power they wield. The concepts in this book provide a solution for this general condition.

THE TRADITIONAL PARADIGM OF MANAGEMENT AND NONMANUFACTURING ORGANIZATIONS

Many who are not involved in manufacturing may ask, "Does this really apply to me or my organization? After all, we don't manufacture." Our knowledge structures should not keep us from understanding how influential the traditional management paradigm has been in contemporary organizations.

The traditional paradigm applies to service organizations, such as hotels, just as surely as it applies to traditional manufacturing firms (Figure 3.8). It can also apply to a package delivery organization, the U.S. Postal Service, and

TRADITIONAL HIERARCHY

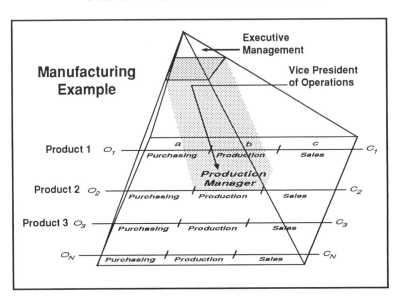

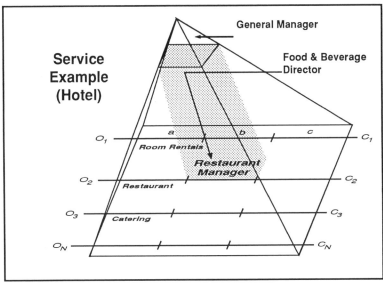

Figure 3.8

any other private or public organization.

Of course, no two organizations are exactly alike. If your organization is typical, it will be easier to say, "this doesn't apply to my organization" than to understand how and why it is applicable. By rejecting applicability, you can avoid the psychological dissonance of examining the need to make profound changes in your organization and in your own personal behavior. It is a general condition that most people find it difficult to make analogies between their own world and concepts in which they have little personal experience or understanding.

The traditional paradigm of management that originated in the manufacturing sector has become the conceptual foundation upon which all management systems and organizations are based. Jet aircraft and propeller-driven planes are significantly different from one another; however, both are subject to the physical laws governing flight. Although small service firms and large manufacturing organizations are different from one another, both spring from the traditional management paradigm.

It is also a general condition that when the impact may be painful, most people will fail to make analogies from areas outside their own. A subsequent general condition is that those who fail to recognize the need to make such analogies and the necessary adjustments are not to be counted among the winners.

General conditions require general solutions. There are no exceptions. Individuals must determine if they are capable of improving their abilities to process information so that existing knowledge structures can be replaced by others more consistent with observable reality. If they cannot, their success in the organization is likely to be bleak.

Here is where chaos theory indicates that: *increasingly, the facts demand that leaders have the courage to face the implications and take appropriate actions.*

The major upheavals taking place as organizations struggle for survival is proof that the entire system needs change. The facts demand that we have a new paradigm of management that can resolve the general paradigmatic problems plaguing organizations. Your organization's prosperity and ultimate survival depends on it!

Chapter 4

Shifting Paradigms of Management

The world hates change, yet it is the only thing that has brought progress.

— Charles Kettering

We should not be surprised that people expect the status quo to continue. Virtually everything we know about the interaction between knowledge structures and paradigms suggests that people's resistance to change is a general condition. Central to the general condition, ideas and concepts are accepted or rejected based on empirical observation and hypothesis testing within a known framework. Therefore, data collected within a paradigm will always support that particular paradigm.

Commander Ward Parker, Jr., of the U.S. Navy wrote: "Of course, no one really knows whether the critical juncture of a paradigm shift is taking place or not. After it occurs, observers can look back at the transition process with the clear and discerning vision of hindsight. But until a shift has actually occurred, people normally think that the status quo will continue, at least for the near future."[1]

Prior to understanding the Copernican model, people looked at the heavens and determined that the stars were moving. If in doubt, the observation could be verified by asking others what they saw. All conventional observations supported the premise that the stars and planets circled the Earth, which was "empirically verified" as the sole stable object at the center of the universe.

Today, this scenario would verify the new paradigm instead of the old. It is interesting that the same phenomena can cause us to reach extremely different conclusions.

Interpretation of data is not simply a function of intelligence. It is more a function of the interactions between knowledge structures and paradigms.

Commander Parker answered a critical and fundamental question when he wrote:

"...What should one look for to determine if the current paradigm ... is becoming outmoded? Basically, the paradigm begins to break down. In other words, there is a persistent failure of the problems of [organizations] to work out as they should. The paradigm no longer provides an adequate explanation or answer to problems, and [organizations experience] an insecurity that slowly but steadily erodes the acceptability of the paradigm."[2]

EVOLVING PARADIGMS

As long as paradigms can be enriched and modified to provide adequate explanations, answers, and predictions, they remain viable.

Remember that a paradigm rests on one fundamental premise. In the Geocentric model, the fundamental premise was that the Earth was the center of the universe around which all heavenly bodies moved. From this simple premise, a complex set of theories and models evolved to explain in more detail how the universe functioned. Additional explanations were required to respond to questions that challenged these theories.

Over the centuries, the answers to increasingly difficult problems began to be based more on faith in the existing paradigm than on actual fact. The paradigm became so theoretically ornate that it began to collapse under its own weight.

Significant paradigmatic shifts are not trivial events. They cause upheaval and pain for some, but bring unprecedented benefits for others—especially those who recognize the future implications of the new paradigm.

A paradigm is based on a simple premise and becomes more complex as problems emerge. The traditional management paradigm has led to multi-layered, top-heavy, slow-to-change organizations unable to provide the value their customers demand. It cannot provide the answers needed to cope with the problems of Endemic Overcapacity in the dynamic chaos of the global economic arena.

THE ERODING ACCEPTABILITY OF THE TRADITIONAL MANAGEMENT PARADIGM

The traditional management paradigm is based on a premise that seemed obvious at the time of its development. It focused almost exclusively on the economics of production rather than on the economics of distribution.

The potential demand for increased production was easily realized as the price of consumer goods fell. The situation was characterized by Jean Baptiste Say, a French economist. Say's Law, which states that supply creates its own demand, holds that theoretically there is an endless cycle:

+ Increases in production reduce unit costs and require more labor
+ Reduced costs and labor put more money into circulation
+ More money creates more buying power and leads to more production

The evolution of the traditional management paradigm was profoundly influenced by Say's Law, which remains valid today in certain circumstances. For example, when newly developed products and services are in the growth phase of their life cycle, increased volume can significantly lower prices and expand effective demand. We have seen this happen with succeeding generations of computer chips.

The learning curve pricing theory is founded on Say's Law. Proponents believe that costs decrease over time because increased volume helps the organization learn to operate more efficiently. To gain a competitive edge, the organization can set prices lower than the current costs because the increased volume will expand applications of its products or services. This expansion of demand takes the organization down the learning curve faster, to the point where the loss-leader becomes profitable. Competitors find it difficult to break into the market because of start-up costs.

Because Say's Law worked in the past, organizations became obsessed with the idea that increased volume meant increased sales. This "more, better, faster" mentality was one of the defining characteristics of the traditional management paradigm.

This mentality has become the panacea for many social and economic woes: the greater the volume, the more people will be employed, and the more money will be available to purchase products and services. Because output is paramount, changes in economic and industrial policy are judged by how much output is increased.

Unfortunately, there is a fundamental flaw with this reasoning. Increased volume will lead to the desired outcome only when that output has consumable value.

In the early stages of industrialization, consumption was a given. Because there was a basic need for food, shelter, and clothing, increased production did increase demand. When basic needs are met, there will still be, for a time, enormous latent demand for luxury items. If prices can be lowered (usually through mass production resulting in lower unit costs), demand follows the increased availability. In these situations, Say's Law is absolutely correct. However, in today's world, which is characterized by Endemic Overcapacity, Say's Law often does not apply.

When production is the primary focus, the customer is secondary. Modern organizations operating in the old paradigm are ruled by internal needs rather than by consumer desires. Tasks take on a life of their own and the customer is ignored.

THE MARKETING VIEW

In the last 50 years, it has become increasingly obvious that customers' needs are the ultimate driving force for economic success. Modern marketing evolved to fill the gap left by the traditional paradigm. Marketing is nothing more than the *natural evolutionary organizational response to Endemic Overcapacity.*

As Endemic Overcapacity spread throughout the world, marketing gained steadily in importance. In 1961, Peter Drucker wrote: "Until the customer has derived final utility, there is really no 'product;' there are only 'raw materials.' And the 'marketing view' looks at the business as directed toward the satisfaction of a customer want and as a purveyor of a customer utility."[3]

Similarly, in a classic article, Theodore Levitt said: "When viewed in (such) a broad context, marketing is a force that should pervade the entire firm. It must enter into the thinking and behavior of all decision makers, regardless of their level within the organization and their functional area. If such is not the case, then...the company will be merely a series of pigeon-holed parts, with no consolidating sense of purpose or direction."[4]

A representative marketing book of the early 1970s introduces the "marketing concept" and defines marketing's role as: "... specifying what products or services with what attributes are wanted by what group of consumers..."[5] The authors of these and similar texts contend that basing decisions on meeting customers' needs is a very difficult concept to operationalize. In other words, it is easier said than done. The weakness of the marketing concept is not in its desirability, but in its implementation. The problem is not what the consumer wants, but how to deliver it.

The set of organizational philosophies that form the basis of the marketing concept also address the concept referred to as quality management—which offers the following benefits:

- Concern about market needs rather than products allows firms to take advantage of opportunities as they arise
- The total operation must be considered in an integrated manner, rather than as isolated departments
- Satisfying customers' needs and wants ensures profitability and survival

Two facts point out the old paradigm's inability to cope with Endemic Overcapacity:

- Special arrangements must be made to attempt to adapt the traditional paradigm to the needs of the distribution function, rather than only to production.
- Despite establishing new departmental functions and reorganizing old ones, the fundamental premise of the traditional paradigm leads to trade-offs and difficulties that cannot be resolved.

The classic marketing text describes this paradigmatic dilemma as follows:

"...Basing important decisions on customer needs is a difficult policy to make operational, especially where important profits are at stake. There are many reasons for this difficulty.

"First and foremost, consumers frequently do not know what they want, or—equally important—they cannot articulate their needs in a way that is meaningful to the business firm, which must have specifics in order to design new products or modify old ones. The vocabulary of the consumer is often unintelligible to an engineer.

"Second, many consumers do not know what they want until they are presented with specific choices.

"Third, many consumers are inconsistent in stating their preferences and needs. They request, directly or indirectly, product features that are incompatible. They want, for example, durability coupled with lower cost, or product versatility with more simplicity.

"Fourth, consumer preferences vary widely."[6]

GROWING INSECURITY

By the mid-1970s, Western organizations began to understand that something was not quite right with economic trends. Firms that had dominated domestic and foreign markets were losing market share at increasing rates. Productivity growth in the American economy as a whole, once among the highest in the world, had become almost stagnant.

By the latter half of the 1970s, the quest for improvement began to take on increased emphasis and visibility. By 1980, the search for productivity had reached such a level of intensity that a major television network developed and aired the prime-time documentary, "If Japan Can...Why Can't We?" Although the documentary was not popular with the general public, it provided U.S. industry with a widespread introduction to the concepts of quality management. Managers were intrigued enough to pursue the notion that quality, productivity, and reliability are complementary rather than mutually exclusive. Understanding the positive relationship between high quality production and lower overall production costs led some firms to concentrate efforts on improving quality and reliability to attain higher productivity. Higher quality with lower costs implies increased value for the customer and greater customer satisfaction. Achieving lasting and continuous improvement in quality, reliability, customer satisfaction, and profitability requires more than a heightened interest and recognition of their importance and interdependence.

The traditional management paradigm's inability to meet the needs of modern organizations is further illustrated by the plethora of management tools that seem to be coming and going at an ever-increasing rate (Figure 4.1). This sincere and frantic quest for new tools and solutions for managing old problems is clear evidence that the old paradigm is flawed.

EVERCHANGING STREAM OF MANAGEMENT TOOLS

ABC (Activity Based Costing)
Accountability and Responsibility
Annual Appraisals
Benchmarking
Brainstorming
Business Process Improvement
Concurrent Engineering
Conforming to Specifications
Conglomeration
Continuous Flow Manufacturing
Cost of Quality
Customer Satisfaction
Cycle Time
Data Banks
Design of Experiments
Diversification
Divestiture
Downsizing
DRP (Distribution Resource Planning)
Employee Participation
Empowerment
Flowcharting
FMEA (Failure Mode/Effects Analysis)
Gap Analysis
Hoshin Planning
Job Posting
Just In Time Inventory
Just In Time Manufacturing
Kaizen Teian 1
Kaizen Teian 2
Kanban
MBO (Management by Objectives)
MBWA (Management by Walking Around)

Management Information Systems
Matrix Management
Mission Statements
Networking
Participative Management
Performance Management
Poka Yoke
Problem Solving
QFD (Quality Function Deployment)
Quality Circles
Quality of Work Life
Quality Partnerships
Quality Tools
Recognition Banquets
Reengineering
Restructuring
Rewards and Recognition
Rightsizing
Root Cause Analysis
Six Sigma
SPC (Statistical Process Control)
Spend Them Into Oblivion
Streamlining
Taguchi Methods and Techniques
Takeovers
Team Building
Total Quality Control
TQM (Total Quality Management)
Value Statements
Vertical Integration
Vision Statements
Zero Defects
Zero Stock

Figure 4.1

Today's organizations are experiencing early shock waves of the shift from the traditional management paradigm. The only way you can be sure that one paradigm is more effective than another is to compare performance. Organizations adopting the new paradigm are indeed performing better than those still employing the old paradigm.

UNDER THE SPELL OF THE QUALITY GURUS

The problems with improving quality and productivity were highlighted by the author of an article in *Fortune* magazine at the peak of the quality awareness fad. With tongue-in-cheek, the author reviewed major quality philosophers of the day (whom he labeled "gurus"), and the problems clients were having implementing their ideas:

> "The gurus seem to agree on certain basic points. They believe that until top management gets permanently involved in quality, nothing will work. They set little store by robots, automation, and other gadgetry. They have little use for quality circles, except as an adjunct to other methods. But beyond these basics, it is every guru for himself.
>
> "Their methods differ markedly...and the whole field is suffused with a fog of jargons, slogans, and

statistics. As a result, the quality message often fails to get through to clients. But when it does, the effects can be remarkable." [7]

In the subhead of the article, the author summarized his findings: "If only the wise men could agree on how to do it." One could editorialize further by saying, "If only the wise men could agree on exactly what it is."

The emergence of modern marketing was the first clear indication that the traditional paradigm was beginning to falter. But the marketing concept, sound in principle and purpose, often failed to succeed because superimposing a new philosophy and functional department based on the traditional paradigm simply could not work.

Similarly, other new management tools, fads, and solutions represented well-intentioned efforts to improve organizational performance. Some efforts have led to lasting improvements, while others have led to little improvement and have left cynicism in their wake. People in many organizations have become accustomed to *programme du jour.*

None of the new tools or solutions, including the now-famous concept of Total Quality Management (TQM), have proven to be a panacea. Criticisms have mounted and the search has intensified to find a miracle cure for organizational ills.

Here are examples of failures in implementation:

+ A survey of 500 American manufacturing service firms found that only 30% felt their total quality programs were having a "significant impact" on the bottom line.[8]
+ In Britain, a survey of 100 companies revealed that 80% said their quality initiatives had not produced any tangible long-term results.[9]
+ Throughout the world, over 75% of organizations have something they believe is a quality initiative in place, but about two-thirds of these efforts grind to a halt in less than two years.[10]

Many organizations that claim to have fallen off the quality wagon were never really on it. Companies that say they are quality oriented and then produce dismal results are unable to give concrete evidence of fundamental changes in their structure or methodology for doing business. *The degree of change in the organization is the principle difference between those that have made great gains through the tools, philosophies, and methods of quality management, and those that have not.*

Total Quality Management has been difficult to implement because too often it represents yet another effort to patch up the traditional paradigm rather than adopt a new and better one. However, the fundamental difference between TQM and its predecessors is that within it are the seeds to understanding the new management paradigm's foundations.

THE FUNDAMENTAL PREMISE OF THE NEW PARADIGM

When a paradigm shift occurs, the best of the old paradigm organizations often fall victim to unknown upstarts who are using the new paradigm.

Japan's ability to produce high-quality, low-cost goods resulted in fact-finding trips to Japan looking for "it." Fact finders came back with various conclusions. Since they did not know "it," most could not see "it." They saw what they <u>thought</u> they should see. Some saw statistical methods being applied and suggested that we use statistics the same way the Japanese did. Others saw quality circles, and still others saw robots. The observers' cognitive processes interpreted what they saw based on their own backgrounds and not on what was really happening.

Collective meocentrism was working overtime when many decided, on the basis of strictly anecdotal evidence, that Americans actually taught the Japanese how to be excellent. They surmised it was really Western methodologies that were succeeding, but the Japanese were actually implementing them. Therefore, if anyone would listen to the same "gurus," they too could create quality and productivity miracles.

The Japanese had stumbled onto the basics of an entirely new business paradigm, but did not recognize the fundamental differences between the old and new. Most incorrectly believed that the uniqueness of their own Japanese culture accounted for the surprisingly good performance of many Japanese firms.

The excellent Japanese firms that came into prominence later—such as Toyota—adopted much of this different paradigm. Successful firms achieved high-quality, low-cost systems by fostering cooperation with their suppliers rather than the conflict-oriented approaches typical of Western firms. The Japanese model was based more on producing a global optimum through customer service and retention than on local optimization of internal production.

The premise of the new management paradigm is the pursuit of the global optimum through holistic processes and systems rather than through organizational and individual specialization. The very foundation upon which a new paradigm must be built is the concept of process and process management.

It is a general condition that managers naturally try to retain the old while adopting the new. To make the transition to the new paradigm, leaders must completely abandon old ideas and concepts. The fundamental characteristics of the traditional paradigm of management and its associated hierarchical management system make it virtually impossible to adapt it to the new paradigm.

Profound behavioral change is required. Both the organization itself and its members must undergo change of major proportions. This requires a thorough and complete cultural change in every sense of the word.

Chapter 5

Changing Organizational Culture

Most managers manage for yesterday's conditions, because yesterday is where they got their experiences and had their successes. But management is about tomorrow, not yesterday.

— Theodore Levitt

The last quarter century has seen a rush to attempt new and different solutions to the unsolvable problems of the traditional management paradigm. When a paradigm is no longer adequate, new elements are sometimes grafted onto the old. The grafted branch may grow and bear fruit. It may even lead to a bigger harvest, but will never perform as well as it could because the traditional paradigm will always limit its potential.

Without paradigmatic change, the very nature of the old stifles and eventually chokes out the new. Because organizational culture is about human behavior, changing management paradigms is far more difficult than changing the more logical and rational scientific paradigms.

ORGANIZATIONAL CULTURE: WHAT IS IT?

Culture is not simply the climate or feelings of the members of a group—it is the <u>behavior</u> of the group and its individual members. This behavior is reflected in the way the organization's members interact with customers, vendors, and other stakeholders; manage the operating environment; perform under stress; cope with change; and pursue excellence.

An organization's culture is both a cause and a consequence of the way people behave. There is a circular flow of mutual causation among organizational behavior, success, and culture. Where cause and effect are circular, there is no top or bottom, and no beginning or end. The organization behaves a certain way, and this behavior is the primary determinant of the organization's overall success. An organization's success, or lack of success, affects its culture, which in turn affects behavior (Figure 5.1).

One might wonder why two separate parts of the same organization can be so different, even though they are similar in design and expected to perform equally well. Inconsistencies in organizational culture or climate are often used to explain differences. If cultural differences explain <u>everything</u>, culture becomes a cliché and contributes very little in the way of understanding. Therefore, we are interested in culture only to the extent that it explains organizational behavior and performance.

MUTUAL CAUSATION AMONG ORGANIZATIONAL CULTURE, BEHAVIOR, AND SUCCESS

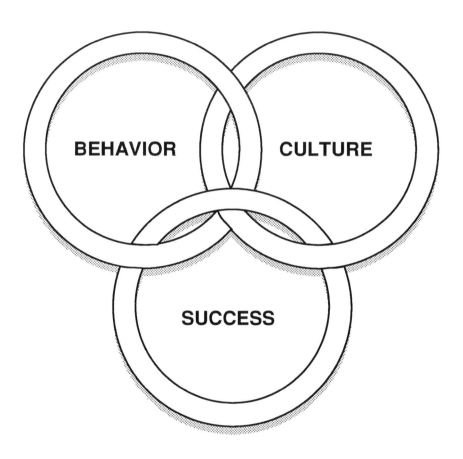

Figure 5.1

Organizational Culture: A Practical Model

A model of organizational culture must be sufficiently complete, robust, and precise to enable us to:

(a) begin with a list of specific and measurable objectives
(b) design an organization that will satisfy these criteria
(c) compare the current organization with the future state to determine what must change
(d) understand how to make these changes (Figure 5.2)

The model of culture we have developed has evolved from our experiences with several hundred organizations of varying size, from public and private sectors, from both manufacturing and service industries, and from countries around the world. It has withstood the test of time and has proven to be useful as well as practical.

The Five Interactive Dimensions of Organizational Culture

An organization's culture has typically been presumed to be little more than its shared beliefs, values, and attitudes. These elements are certainly important. However, a deeper

MODEL OF ORGANIZATIONAL CULTURE

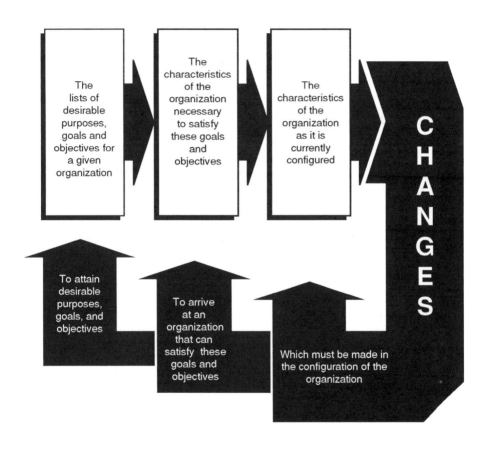

Figure 5.2

look reveals that an organization's culture is instead comprised of the following five components:

+ Organizational structure
+ Shared beliefs, values, attitudes, and traditions
+ Language and patterns of communication
+ Technologies and their applications
+ Patterns of leadership

The "wheel" of organizational culture illustrates the dynamic interactions among all five of these fundamental dimensions. Notice that shared beliefs, values, and attitudes are not the center of the model—structure is the core dimension (Figure 5.3).

This model of culture is analogous to considering a gyroscope as the heart of the organization's guidance system. The ability to reach the objective depends on the correct and coordinated functioning of the guidance system.

Structure is the key stabilizing dimension of culture. It transforms abstract dimensions, such as beliefs and values, into concrete forms and patterns of behavior. The structure of an organization includes the relationships among line and staff workers, functions and markets, vendors and distribution channels, and labor and management. The structure is based on social institutions, formal and informal relationships, and politics.

ORGANIZATIONAL CULTURE WHEEL

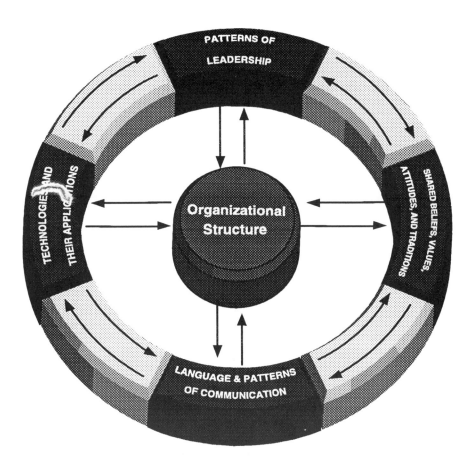

The arrows indicate simultaneous interaction and causation around the outside of the wheel and between the core and the outer dimensions.

Figure 5.3

In planning the organization's future, leaders must first determine (or examine) the mission and vision, then they must decide how to achieve them. In theory, vision and mission dictate goals and objectives, which, in turn, dictate strategies, which determines structure. In practice we often find that the existing structure is resistant to change, so that rather than structure following strategy (the correct way), structure limits strategy and objectives. As a result, goals can become unobtainable.

The resistance to change inherent in most social systems comes from the interaction of structure with the inertia of the status quo. If an organization is determined to simultaneously improve its performance and its customer satisfaction, the resulting actions will affect all the dimensions of culture. Each aspect of culture is critical to the whole, but the whole is more than the sum of the parts. Strength in one dimension will not compensate for weakness in another. For example, having an ideal structure will not overcome serious deficiencies in any of the other four dimensions, but the wrong structure will thwart any attempts to significantly change the organization's culture through any or all of the others. An organization must be willing to make necessary changes in all five dimensions, especially structure if significant planned cultural change is to succeed.

Organizational Structure

Structure is not simply an organizational chart. It is the social system upon which the organization is based. Some societies are based on nuclear families, some on extended families, and others on a combination of the two. In the same way, organizations have building-block subgroups. The interrelationships of these groups influence, and are influenced by, the other four cultural dimensions.

The relationship between the work process and the functional structure is complex (Figure 5.4). If you fit the structure to the process, organizational problems such as coordination and communications are reduced. However, if you start with a structure and try to adapt the process to it, problems such as the relationships between groups and individuals are compounded. These interactions and relationships between people in an organization are often referred to as politics.

Politics can provide a mechanism to force evolutionary changes in the organization's structure, and can help individuals adapt to authority. The prospect of drastic change carries with it uncertainty, and the resulting dissonance often manifests itself in the form of increased political behavior. Politics are too often used to pursue individual advantage, obtain additional power, and preserve the status quo.

Organizational Structure

- Relationships:
    - work and structure
    - among groups
    - among individuals
    - among individuals and groups

- Patterns of personal and organizational authority, influence, and power

- Personnel selection, retention, and development

- The role of education and training

- Other

Figure 5.4

Excessive politics usually result from one of two conditions. When too many areas of responsibility conflict and no smooth mechanisms exist to resolve the conflicts, the internal concerns become incompatible with the organization's mission. The result is often over-staffing in the mid-management ranks.

The second condition that encourages organizational politics exists when an organization's decisions are being made without facts. When subjective considerations like personal relationships and favoritism supersede facts, organizational politics run rampant. The organization's mission is thwarted, while both the customer and internal performance suffer.

The dynamics of power and authority determine the way people are selected and developed. For example, if an organization tends to be very hierarchical, its successful associates are probably very different from those in an organization that emphasizes autonomy and personal accountability.

Organizations can fall victim to a self-fulfilling prophecy: "We can't get the kind of people who can assume responsibility." In fact, they can. When people enter an organization, they must be educated and trained in the fundamentals of the new cultural and social systems. This knowledge enables them to readily adapt to the new systems and contributes to high performance.

Behavior is a more reliable predictor of beliefs, values, and attitudes than these constructs are of behavior. What, then, does that mean for organizational culture and behavior? In practical terms, it means that if people are required to behave inconsistently with their beliefs, values, and attitudes, they will experience a state of psychological stress referred to as dissonance. For example, if a manager values customer satisfaction, but the organization's policies and processes prevent this, he or she will experience dissonance. There are three proactive ways to reduce this dissonance and regain a state of psychological comfort.

First, remove oneself from the situations that cause conflict. In an organization, this means resigning, asking for a transfer, or changing employment status. Second, one can become an "organizational cynic" by rationalizing the disparity between personal values and required behavior.

For example, consider the case of a manager who arranged for an investment in new technology and training to increase long-term results. Then an organization-wide reduction in expenses destroyed the long-term improvement efforts. Later, over a few drinks with colleagues, everyone agreed how foolish these cutbacks were and how, if this continues, they were all going to be in deep trouble. In spite of that, the next day they all returned to work and carried out the cost-reduction directives. Each reduced his or her own dissonance by projecting frustrations onto the organization and its leadership. They preserved their ability to continue in the organization by separating beliefs, values, and attitudes from on-the-job behavior. This type of organizational cynicism is the reason many organizations cannot seem to overcome the status quo. Although messages are heard, actions are carefully moderated to avoid conflict between beliefs, values, attitudes, and expected behavior patterns.

Third, beliefs, values, and attitudes will change to accommodate expected behavior. Those associates willing and able to embrace change will emerge with an aligned set of behaviors, values, and attitudes. Therefore, training must be designed to force behavioral changes congruent with the organizational structure if the organization is truly dedicated to changing its culture. Military organizations have traditionally understood and practiced these principles since before the dawn of recorded history. Without behavioral change there will be no cultural change.

Shared Beliefs, Values, Attitudes, and Traditions

The intangible beliefs, values, and attitudes of individuals interest us only if they are in some way related to our true concern—manifested behavior. A baseline set of beliefs, values, and attitudes that should be of importance to virtually any organization is shown in Figure 5.5. Some organizations might add items, and others might discount

Shared Beliefs, Values, Attitudes, and Traditions

- Sense of purpose

- Focus on the customer

- Commitment to excellence

- Importance of the long term

- Traditional bureaucratic versus participative decision making and risk taking

- Sense of personal accountability and responsibility

- Willingness to change

- Sense of urgency

- Other

Figure 5.5

the items listed. The list is intended to provide a basis for understanding and introspection. It is not intended to be exhaustive. That is why it ends with "other."

Sense of Purpose

One of the central constructs around which many beliefs, values, and attitudes revolve is the organization's shared sense of purpose. When the sense of purpose acts as a clarifying and motivating construct, it is well understood and consistent with the culture. For example, if the purpose of the organization is to deliver packages on time every time and "on time" is precisely defined, everyone's efforts can be focused on the same target. Similarly, if the purpose of a trauma center is to save lives, properly completing insurance forms prior to admission must be a secondary priority.

If individuals share the organization's sense of purpose, they will behave accordingly. A shared sense of purpose is both a cause and a consequence of attaining and maintaining organizational alignment.

Focus on the Customer

Few organizations would indicate they are not interested in satisfying their customers. Yet we have all seen sharp differences between apparently similar organizations when it comes to actually serving and trying to satisfy their customers "one at a time," rather than en masse. For example, in the event of foul weather or mechanical difficulties, one airline may go out of its way to assist its inconvenienced passengers while another will make only minimum efforts.

It is easy for any organization to say that its customers are important, but attitudes and actions—not public relations and advertising—reflect the truth. In the preceding airline example, the actions of the associates who are only expected to do the minimum to aid passengers reflects the organization's lack of focus on its customers and their satisfaction. When an organization tries to satisfy and retain its existing customers while trying to attract new ones, it expects and rewards a different kind of behavior than if it is more concerned about short-term factors. The associates of the organization know the truth and it will be reflected in their shared beliefs, values, and attitudes.

Commitment to Excellence

When an organization and each of its associates are sincerely focused on group and individual excellence, measures of organizational performance are taken seriously and performance is viewed with pride. Individual behavior will reflect how seriously the organization is committed to excellence.

Commitment to excellence involves an array of key concepts that can influence the way everything is done. Questions such as the following are critical:

- Who established the specifications for the outputs— the organization or the customer?
- Does the organization operate according to internal specifications or its customers' requirements and expectations?
- How good is good enough?
- Does the organization knowingly ship inferior products or provide poor service?
- Does the organization meet delivery dates and other commitments?
- Does the organization strive for continuous improvement?
- Does the organization tolerate waste?

Neither words nor quality statements indicate a commitment to excellence. A commitment is reflected in the way everyone responds to opportunities to reduce waste and make improvements affecting external customers and enhancing overall performance.

Importance of the Long Term

How long is long term? First-rate Asian firms view the long term as 10 years or longer. North American competitors behave as if a quarter of a year were the long term and consider the fourth quarter truly long term because it makes the year. How do long- and short-term goals interact? In too many organizations long-term goals exist on paper, but the short term is little more than a firefighting operation. How the long term is viewed can determine the entire success of the organization. Questions such as which markets are targeted, which products are developed, what is researched, and how problems are solved within the organization are very much dependent upon the organization's concept of the long term.

Traditional Bureaucracy Versus Participative Decision Making and Risk Taking

Most traditional organizations are bureaucracies where authority and responsibility flow from the top down to different levels of managers. These organizations tend to be functionally oriented (down the columns). Coordination between functions is provided by management.

Key decisions in bureaucracies are usually made several levels above where they have immediate and direct impact. Decision makers rely on information gathered by staff specialists, who collect and process the data, organize the resulting information, study the various alternative choices, and make recommendations. Frequently in bureaucracies those who are intimately involved with the work do not participate in this data collection, analysis, or decision making.

We are seeing continued acceptance of the concept that the people who know the most about a process are those who work on that process. This movement, often referred to as "participative management," has taken many forms. It has succeeded in some organizations and failed entirely in others.

Participative is not synonymous with democratic. Participative management requires a system in which employees at every level have both the *right* and the *obligation* to provide insight and feedback. This input enables associates to do their jobs better, quicker, and more cost effectively. In order for this system to work, leaders must listen and respond in a way that is in the organization's best interest.

Participative decision making places a high value on risk taking and individual initiative. The organization must determine how to evaluate and reward team and individual performance. If the organization rewards only individual performance, there is little incentive for teams to excel. However, if group efforts receive significant reward and recognition, the motivation to participate is much greater. Once the appropriate behaviors are required and rewarded, the results will be seen in the shared beliefs and values of the organization.

Sense of Personal Accountability and Responsibility

Personal accountability and responsibility are key to establishing positive values, beliefs, and attitudes in the organization's culture. Employers who foster high levels of personal accountability for performance encourage employees to have higher expectations of themselves, their peers, and their superiors. In an environment of trust, employees are much more likely to take a proactive role in pursuing personal and organizational excellence than if bound by the restrictive measures of a bureaucracy. Contrarily, organizations that prohibit employees from making even the most fundamental decisions or becoming actively involved in their own development severely limit their employees' desire or ability to strive for excellence.

Willingness to Change

Significant change can be critical to an organization's performance and survival. Too often, organizations pride themselves on their willingness to change, but in reality make only superficial changes.

Other organizations have developed a culture that thrives on change for the sake of change. Constant small changes, such as shuffling reporting relationships or launching one new campaign after another, limit the organization's ability to undertake meaningful paradigmatic change.

One of the most critical needs in many organizations is to develop a shared definition of what real change is and how the organization will implement it.

In ancient times, Petronius Arbiter recognized the difference between real change and the appearance of change. In describing the Roman Army, he said:

"We trained hard...but it seemed that every time we were beginning to form up into teams we would be reorganized...I was to learn later in life that we tend to meet any new situation by reorganizing, and a wonderful method it can be for creating the illusion of progress while producing confusion, inefficiency, and demoralization..."[1]

Sense of Urgency

An organization's sense of urgency is reflected in how quickly its members respond to opportunities and threats. Organizations that anticipate the need to change, and do so solely on the basis of that need, are culturally different. They are proactive rather than reactive. The willingness to change and take risks is directly related to the value the organization places on the need to act quickly. In today's environment of Endemic Overcapacity, a sense of urgency is critical to an organization's high performance and survival.

Once we establish how the organization should behave, we must align the behavior of its members at all levels. The beliefs, values, and attitudes of those able and willing to change will adjust as necessary to accommodate the expected and rewarded patterns of behavior. Those unable or unwilling to change will have to leave.

Language and Patterns of Communications

Roget defines language as "a system of terms used by a people sharing a history and culture."[2] The language of an organization naturally includes the technical terms specific to the industry, the idiomatic expressions of the geographic region, and internal jargon. When these elements are combined, they convey meaning. However, the receiver often misunderstands the sender's meaning. This frequently happens when senders do not have a clear definition of their target audience.

There are a myriad of reasons for such misunderstandings. When the sender's ideas are not crisp and precise, the message is open to a variety of interpretations. Or, jargon and technical terms may be defined differently by senders and receivers, especially if the communication is between different geographic regions or functional areas.

Even when an organization has a common language without geographic or technical barriers, there can still be misunderstandings of common definitions. For example, what is "quality"—that is, at what level of performance do you have quality? How does "good quality" differ from "bad quality?" Differences on this level are a result of meocentrism—imposing our actual experiences on our interpretation of the meaning of words.

The imprecision of language, spoken and written, has brought into play nonverbal communication methods—

LANGUAGE AND PATTERNS OF COMMUNICATION

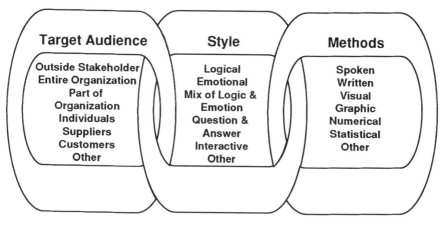

Figure 5.6

visual, graphical, numerical, and most recently, statistical—where a more common ground can be established (Figure 5.6). These language methods or patterns attempt to provide clearer, more concise communication on issues such as what is "good quality" versus "poor quality."

Culture shapes and is shaped by language. French poets express themselves quite differently than do Japanese haikuists. Not only does the syntax vary dramatically, but so does the mental image each communicates. Similarly, computer programmers and mathematicians use a language of logic to communicate, while sales representatives and marketers use the language of persuasion. These differences are obvious; others are more subtle. Often it is communication style—emotional versus logic-driven—that causes managers to spend inordinate amounts of time delivering organizational messages.

Language is a complex and critical cultural factor, and is always changing. It changes not only from society to society, but from generation to generation, decade to decade, and management fad to management fad. New words evolve and old words are redefined to accommodate the ever-changing communication needs of culture.

Technologies and Their Applications

In the broadest sense, technology is applying science and knowledge for practical purpose. The planned and formal application of any technology can be called a technological system. This distinguishes it from a body of knowledge and science that is not applied in a systematic way (Figure 5.7).

The broad area of management, which should be based on science, knowledge, and experience, is a technology. Equipment and physical processes are thought of as traditional technologies, but the way an organization is managed is also a reflection of technology. How an organization is managed includes production and distribution, internal and external communication, performance measurement, resource allocation and planning, and general information systems.

Technologies and Their Applications

- Management

- Production

- Delivery

- Communication

- Customer satisfaction measurement

- Organization performance measurement

- Resource allocation

- Planning

- Information

- Other

Figure 5.7

I have encountered senior managers who casually say they plan to change their management systems. However, they have no specific plans, and have not mapped out a blueprint of the new systems. They may have written a few memos or prepared a few seminars, assuming that the only thing required to accomplish change is simple communication. Meanwhile, the same manager may invest substantial time and effort buying a new piece of equipment. Which should have more impact on the organization: the way it is managed, or adding equipment (even if it is important)?

Contemporary managerial systems attempt to effect managerial control through cost accounting systems. In fact, managerial accounting systems are the resource allocation and evaluation mechanisms of the business. Economics in a broad, general context is the science of resource allocation. But, if economics is a science, why is it so difficult to obtain agreement among economists? It is because various economic models (i.e., theories) are based on a series of assumptions that can produce different conclusions.

Those familiar with costs and accounting will recognize the key role of assumptions. Cost allocation and reporting systems are based on many assumptions that can have a profound impact on our cost estimates and on managerial decisions. The widespread belief that a certain amount of waste is acceptable, and even economically necessary, has a devastating effect on efforts to improve quality, productivity, and customer satisfaction.

Why does such an assumption persist in light of overwhelming evidence to the contrary? Part of the answer lies in the way we measure costs. Consider the following excerpt from a leading management accounting textbook:

"Most production processes generate some bad units along with the good ones, as an *unavoidable* result of the most economical combination of the factors of production. *Although it may be technically possible to eliminate spoilage* altogether in many instances, it may be *uneconomical* to do so. This is because the costs of lowering spoilage rates are greater than the cost of spoilage eliminated.

"Working within the selected set of production conditions, management must establish the rate of spoilage that is to be regarded as normal. Normal spoilage is what arises under *efficient* operating conditions; it is an inherent result of the particular process and is thus *uncontrollable in the short run.* Costs of normal spoilage are typically viewed as a part of the costs of *good production,* because the attaining of good units necessitates the simultaneous appearance of spoiled units. *In other words, normal spoilage is planned spoilage, in the sense that the choice of a*

*given combination of factors of production entails a
spoilage rate that management is willing to accept.*"[3]
[italics added]

The preceding passage was chosen because of the credibility of its author and its representation of the field. The
italics highlight some of the key assumptions upon which
accounting systems are based. One is that bad units are
unavoidable "normal spoilage" in any process. Accepting
normal spoilage as part of the cost of goods is assumed since
"normal spoilage is what arises under efficient operating
conditions." This assumption results from a mistake that
businesses make: pursuing the most economical operation
for the short run. As a result, many managers cannot
understand why quality and productivity problems are
destroying their firms when their operations appear to be as
well managed as in previous years.

Imagine that a process produces one incorrectly colored
pink pen for every two red pens; therefore, normal spoilage
is one pen out of three. Cost reports indicate the total cost to
produce the acceptable red pens is $1.50. If the process is
consistent, the cost data will indicate 75¢ per salable unit.
But when variances occur, an alarm goes off. If suddenly
two pink pens for every two red ones are produced, management will work to regain only the "acceptable norm" of one
pink to two red pens.

Normal spoilage also does not take chaos theory into account. For example, we might find that efforts to minimize the price of purchased materials have led to inconsistent quality in incoming supplies and resulted in higher levels of spoilage. Or, some defective pens pass inspection and go to customers who discard them without telling us, buy replacements from our competition, and never buy from us again. Or, our marketing people misjudge the ink colors our customers want. Or, we design a pen our engineers like, but our customers don't like it. Few of these costs appear directly on a cost-accounting form that shows the true significance and amount of waste. We should be disturbed by how few of these costs associated with failure enter into our decision making.

This simple example leads to several discomforting conclusions:

1. The "true" costs of poor quality are almost always significantly underestimated.
2. Actual unit costs and their composition are almost never accurately estimated.
3. Efforts to minimize costs in one area can negatively affect other areas and increase total costs (if the costs of poor quality are taken into account).
4. Traditional cost information includes a large component of subjective, rather than objective, data.

5. Traditional cost information leads to suboptimal decisions that are often inconsistent with the global optimum.

6. Management measurement systems and controls inhibit our ability to make the decisions and changes necessary to compete in the world markets.

All of the technological systems (Figure 5.7) can be adversely affected by the fundamental assumptions of the old paradigm. Each must be designed to deliver the information and output necessary to meet the needs of a High Performance Organization.

Patterns of Leadership

Leadership is made up of four interdependent patterns (Figure 5.8). The most basic of these is the ability to create and articulate a viable, compelling vision of the organization, independent of present conditions. To be effective, this vision must be so compelling that the organization's associates agree with and are anxious to actively and sincerely support it.

The second pattern of leadership is the willingness and ability to lead the organization in pursuit of the vision, even when there is reluctance to do so. Significant change is never easy, particularly for those who prefer the comfort of the status quo. Effective leaders implement their organization's vision in spite of resistance.

Patterns of Leadership

- Creation and articulation of a viable and compelling organizational vision

- Willingness and ability to compel the organization and its associates to pursue that vision

- Willingness and ability to act swiftly, decisively, and with force when required

- Capability to effectively manifest practical leadership through:
    - Style
    - Dramatics
    - Folklore
    - Symbolism
    - Constancy of themes

Figure 5.8

The third pattern of knowing what to do and how to do it is never enough. The willingness to act quickly and forcefully when difficult things must be done is also required. This leadership dimension requires a bit of caution because it is not productive to act quickly without knowing clearly how actions will affect the vision.

The final pattern is a symphony of style, dramatics, folklore, symbolism, and constancy of theme. Great leaders have recognized how to get organizations or nations to perform at higher levels by creating such symphonies.

All four patterns of leadership are essential, and no single one is sufficient in its own right. Only when all come together in an effective and consistent pattern can leadership be effective, especially in a High Performance Organization, which must be prepared to change often and quickly.

In an organization that has not been undergoing significant change, patterns and manifestations of leadership tend to remain stable and predictable. The existing structure, especially the selection of leaders and their indoctrination, ensures the continuation of similar characteristics and behavioral patterns.

Major changes in an organization's culture do not just happen. Regardless of why change is needed, the first step is deciding to change. Leaders must alter their visions and beliefs and then lead the adoption of substantially different systems. Unless the structural dimensions of the organization's culture are altered, it will be difficult to make successful changes in the other dimensions.

To maintain course and momentum, an organization should not be exposed to more than a few important themes at any given time. Significant change represents a major theme. Such themes should not be perceived as fleeting and superficial in nature. They must be emphasized and constantly supported by the organization's leaders.

CONCLUSION

Organizational culture is vitally important. Our brief discussion of culture and its dimensions highlights both the complexity and dynamic nature.

When an organization's culture is allowed to develop and change on its own, chaos theory can be applicable. Seemingly unnoticeable ripples in any of the five dimensions of culture lead to events that cannot be predicted with linear models or thought processes. The same initial stimulus in identical complex systems will not necessarily lead to the same results.

Therefore, to understand organizational culture, we must first recognize that it is a complex system. When we realize that the organization's culture and success are intertwined and interdependent, it should be clear that we must be prepared to plan for, create, and maintain the appropriate culture. That is, we must be willing to implement organizational change with the full knowledge of the complex nature of the systems involved (Figure 5.9).

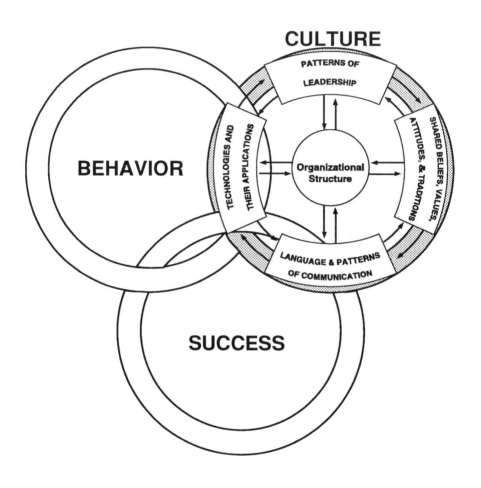

Figure 5.9

Management must plan the required cultural changes if the organization is to successfully adopt a new paradigm. These changes will involve all five dimensions of organizational culture. The plan must be carefully constructed and well thought out, with ample provision for coordination and mid-course corrections.

Once a leadership group has accepted the need to change the organization and to effect a paradigm shift, the next step is to fully understand the new paradigm and its implications. Leadership must then wholeheartedly embrace the effort, develop a plan of action, provide the necessary resources, and lead the change.

Organizations that are in the forefront of embracing the new paradigm of the fast, focused, and flexible High Performance Organization will be tomorrow's leaders. The five dimensions of culture are very much like the compelling analogy presented by the great Chinese strategist, Sun Tzu:[4]

- ◆ The musical notes are only five in number but their melodies are so numerous that one cannot hear them all.
- ◆ The primary colors are only five in number but their combinations are so infinite that one cannot visualize them all.

The implications for leaders and managers should be clear. It is up to them to compose the melodies and paint the pictures.

CHAPTER 6

INTRODUCTION TO THE HIGH PERFORMANCE ORGANIZATION

If you want to be the greatest organization, you have to start acting like one today.

– Tom Watson, Sr.

Many organizations are unable to cope or compete in today's dynamic global markets. This is primarily a function of an obsolete management paradigm. The general solution for this general condition requires implementation of a new paradigm of management that addresses the following weaknesses and limitations of its predecessor:

♦ The inability to maintain a clear focus on customers' dynamic requirements
♦ Limited ability to maintain high levels of performance excellence, while pursuing long-term customer satisfaction
♦ Management systems that limit, rather than enhance, performance
♦ A focus on internal organizational issues rather than external markets and competition

The structure of a High Performance Organization is based on a hierarchy of systems and processes. This structure allows the organization to focus on optimizing customer satisfaction, while maintaining excellence in other performance measures, particularly cash flow, long-term profitability, market share, and margins. To attain and maintain focus on operational excellence requires fast and flexible responses to change. The traditional paradigm cannot ensure that organizations will sustain high performance over time; however, the new paradigm guarantees the flexibility to meet long-term requirements.

"Out of the Box" One More Time

The framework of existing knowledge structures can easily inhibit management's ability to comprehend the essence of the new paradigm. The term "out-of-the-box thinking" is a cliché regularly used by managers. Its overuse does not make it any less valid.

Too often we find managers who are vocal about the need for new thinking trapped in their own boxes. They encourage others to get out of the box, but they themselves continue without personal change. Some so-called change gurus have been working from the same set of notes for at least 10 years. The only way to determine whether you are in or out of the box is through observation by someone outside your organization that you trust to tell you the truth. For most of us, this "truth" is difficult to accept.

THE FOUNDATIONS OF THE NEW PARADIGM OF MANAGEMENT

The new management paradigm rests on the premise that the organization must focus on its customers and on all other aspects of organizational performance simultaneously. To be *focused* means to concentrate on, study, understand, and respond accordingly. To respond means to change as much and as often as required in a minimum amount of time—that is, to be able to change *fast*. The systems needed to meet and satisfy customer requirements must be designed to avoid suboptimization, and must be *flexible* enough to adjust to external chaos.

ARCHITECTURAL REQUIREMENTS FOR THE NEW PARADIGM

The new high performance management paradigm must meet specific criteria; consequently, individuals' roles may change dramatically. Focusing on satisfying customer requirements and achieving high levels of organizational performance requires the interaction of leadership, people, process management, and systems and structure (Figure 6.1).

KEY CHARACTERISTICS OF THE HIGH PERFORMANCE ORGANIZATION

Focus on Customers and Performance – Customer satisfaction and organizational performance are mutually supportive goals.

Process Management – All work is a process. All processes can benefit from improvement and innovation.

Leadership – Senior management must own the implementation of processes, systems, and structures.

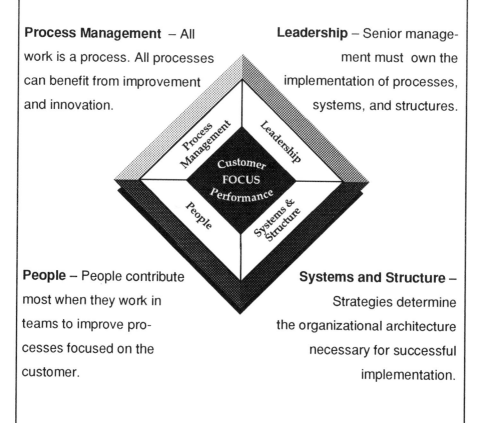

People – People contribute most when they work in teams to improve processes focused on the customer.

Systems and Structure – Strategies determine the organizational architecture necessary for successful implementation.

Figure 6.1

Focus on Customers and Performance

The organization must be constructed so that it can maintain an external focus on:

- Constantly changing customer requirements
- Competitors
- Other relevant economic and market forces and changes

We see culture-based variations in how organizations take care of their customers. Customer focus begins with identifying customers, measuring satisfaction, and discovering the key performance factors that drive their expectations. The key to customer loyalty is complete satisfaction with both product and service.

Organizations must maintain an external focus on anticipating and satisfying customers' changing requirements. The best organizations have sharpened their focus to give customers what they want, when they want it. Home Depot Chief Executive Bernie Marcus says their service philosophy is: "Every customer has to be treated like your mother, your father, your sister, or your brother." Partner, Arthur Blank, adds: "the Holy Grail is...an almost blind, passionate commitment to taking care of customers."[1]

While maintaining its <u>external</u> focus, the organization must also maintain a focus on optimizing its own <u>internal</u>

109

performance. The organization must be constructed and aligned so that it maintains its external focus, while it also focuses on optimizing its internal performance. The organization's performance is not independent of the customer's requirement, but is focused so that improved performance benefits both the customer and the organization. History is full of examples where organizations improved their performance when they concentrated on their core business to more effectively focus on both their own strengths and the customer's needs.

Significant changes in external conditions occur so quickly that, when compared to the past, today's environment is chaotic. All components of the High Performance Organization must have built-in flexibility to cope effectively with external chaos without allowing it to penetrate the organization. An analogy to avoiding organizational chaos is designing buildings to withstand earthquakes by bending with the forces, instead of designing buildings to stand firm and be destroyed.

The focus on organizational performance concentrates on streamlining and redesigning processes across the entire value chain so that unnecessary process steps and functions are eliminated. Every possible action is taken to improve processes that add value.

Process Management

Webster defines "process" as a series of actions or operations conducted to an end. In organizations, all economic outputs are created through processes. The basic level of process is a <u>micro process</u>. Micro processes combine to form <u>processes</u> that in turn combine to form <u>macro processes</u>. Macro processes combine to form <u>systems</u>.

Effectively managing processes requires a systematic approach of process management consisting of four distinct steps.

♦ *Focus—identify an important step in an area of your responsibility*. Identify both customer and management concerns. First, concentrate on meeting customer requirements and the performance criteria imposed by stakeholders. Prioritize significant processes related to these issues.

♦ *Define—clarify what is supposed to be happening*. It is important to reach a common understanding of process flow, determine boundaries of responsibility, establish clear standards, and develop appropriate measures. Management authority is manifested through standards.

♦ *Analyze—determine what is actually happening*. Next analyze process performance relative to key measures and standards. It is critical to recognize that all process and system inputs, activities, and outputs are subject to variation.

♦ *Improve—make it better.* Some process improvements are incremental, others require innovative process redesign. They all focus on continuously enhancing process performance for customer satisfaction.

The customer is a critical monitor of process acceptability. All process modifications must be linked back to constantly changing customer requirements. What is acceptable today may not be acceptable tomorrow. The process must be continuously improved with input from both process operators and process customers.

Any activity, process, or system that does not add value must be eliminated. Simplicity is better than complexity, and less is better than more, particularly when it comes to management systems.

Systems and Structure

A new paradigm organization has two generic types of complementary systems:

♦ Product/Service Delivery Systems (also called Business Systems)—they produce and deliver products and services of value to customers.

◆ Management/Leadership Systems—they are involved in managing the organization.

The systems and the structure in which they are housed must be designed to meet the requirements of the organization's strategies. As strategies change, so must systems and structures—therefore, the continuing need for flexibility.

Each system is a link in the chain from origin to final end user. In some cases, multiple organizations are involved in the value chain, each acting as one link—the supplier, the producer, the shipper, the distributor. When an organization is only one link, it is imperative that partnerships are formed with other links to work together to optimize the end product.

People

General Sherbine of the Royal Saudi Armed Forces concluded his presentation to participants in a Tennessee Associates International seminar in Saudi Arabia by saying, "Quality is you." This simple statement underscores how important the individual is to the success of any organization. People are an integral and indispensable part of processes and systems. The people most likely to be successful in the new paradigm organization have a sense of personal responsibility and accountability. They thrive in a fast-paced, change-oriented, empowered, and cooperative environment.

People require ongoing education and training. They need interactive communication with co-workers, customers, and suppliers to continuously update their skills and mission. Personal growth opportunities are more likely to be horizontal than vertical. Advancement opportunities will be limited because there will be fewer middle managers or staff functions in a new paradigm organization. The best route to personal security and professional growth is skill enhancement and development.

In the new paradigm organization, successful people must understand and become aligned with the organization's vision, mission, and values. Individuals must also be devoted to striving for excellence in both individual and group performance.

Teams provide a major vehicle for organizing people to achieve high performance. Organizing the process so that people can work in teams achieves results. Team participation gets people successfully involved, builds enthusiasm, generates ownership, and results in commitment.

Leadership

Executive leadership must create and articulate a vision of the organization's future. Leaders must have the ability, willpower, and constancy of purpose to move the organization along the path to attain that vision. If the barriers that limit change in the organization are to be overcome, leaders must have the courage, character, and integrity to make tough decisions.

Leaders at all levels must be able and willing to act decisively, swiftly, and with force when required. They must understand the organization's vision and mission and align their areas of responsibility accordingly.

The leaders' authority manifests itself through standards established in the systems and processes they are responsible for. Leaders should create charters that carefully define the boundaries of decision making for those involved in the processes and systems. These charters must be specific, yet broad enough, to permit individuals to fulfill their responsibilities to customers and to other stakeholders.

Among the critical responsibilities of leaders are the following:

- Allocating the resources required for the organization to fulfill the mission
- Creating and maintaining a culture in which the organization is driven to attain and maintain excellence
- Consistently leading by example

A HIERARCHY OF SYSTEMS AND PROCESSES

The new organizational structure must be based on a hierarchy of systems and processes instead of a hierarchy of individuals.

The structure of the new paradigm organization must not be confused with a traditional organization chart that places people in a hierarchy. Systems and processes should not be forced into hierarchical structures based on the strengths and weaknesses of individuals. Instead, the system's requirements should determine where people are placed. The new paradigm structure is a radically different picture of systems and processes—it is not a traditional organizational chart.

THE NEW PARADIGM ORGANIZATION: PRODUCTION AND DELIVERY

The new paradigm organization must effectively apply its resources across processes and systems to produce high quality outputs. In this new paradigm organization, everything is done right the first time, in the simplest, most rational manner; customer needs are met in a timely way, and continuous learning and improvement are achieved in all processes and systems.

The basic component of the organization is the process—a set of activities and interrelated actions that add value to a set of inputs. Processes combine to form product/ service delivery systems of value-added activities (Figure 6.2).

A GENERIC PROCESS

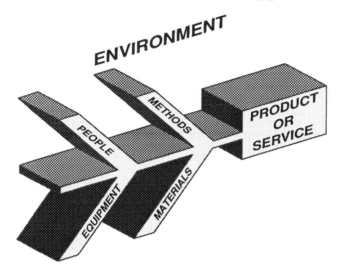

Figure 6.2

Consider a product/service delivery system for pencils. The process begins with the necessary input materials— wood, graphite, eraser, and metal binder. Working backwards along the production chain, we see that each input is the output of other "upstream" production delivery systems. For the wood, the origination is the tree; for the metal and graphite, it is the mine. This set of inputs, from origin to consumer, moves through a product/service delivery system (Figure 6.3).

VALUE CHAIN
PRODUCT/DELIVERY SYSTEM

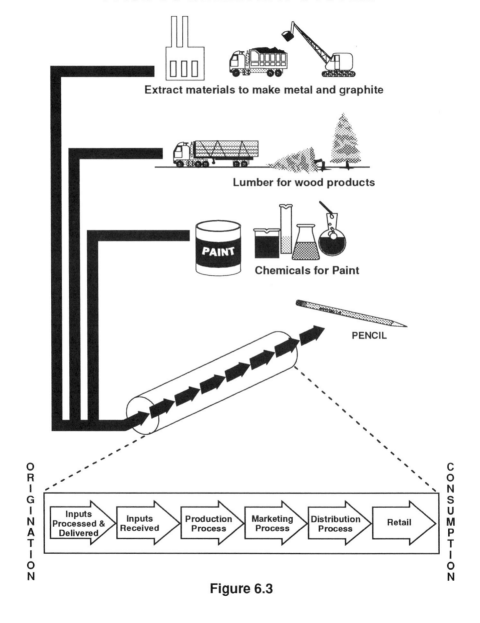

Extract materials to make metal and graphite

Lumber for wood products

PAINT

Chemicals for Paint

PENCIL

| O R I G I N A T I O N | Inputs Processed & Delivered | Inputs Received | Production Process | Marketing Process | Distribution Process | Retail | C O N S U M P T I O N |

Figure 6.3

The pitfalls and wastes of local optimization are avoided through systematic process management. This methodology ensures that process boundaries, linkages, and simultaneous inputs are clearly understood. Both learning and experience assure effective measurement, analysis, and continuous improvement of the individual processes and the entire product/service delivery system.

When the organization is viewed from the perspective of processes and systems, instead of an organizational chart, it becomes clear that each product/service delivery system could be a separate entity or business. We will interchangeably refer to these as business systems (Figure 6.4).

BUSINESS SYSTEMS
(Product/Service Delivery Systems)

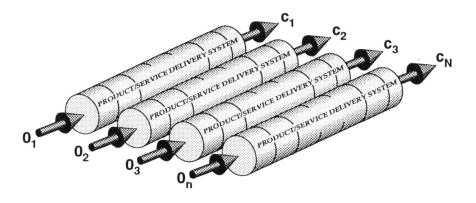

Figure 6.4

Each of the product/service delivery systems should be better able to fulfill its mission when it is part of a combined organization rather than as a stand-alone entity. This synergy is the rationale for combining multiple product/service delivery systems, and creating a more complex organization.

Synergy, where 2 plus 2 equals more than 4, has been the announced purpose of practically every major organizational development fad. Until now, the overall results have not been especially satisfying. Vertical integration, diversification, conglomeration, divestiture, and many other efforts have been launched with great expectations. They were found wanting and were replaced, only to see the same cycle repeat itself. One of the general conditions that explains why expected synergies are rarely achieved is the fundamental inability of the traditional paradigm to permit attainment of the global optimums necessary to produce synergy.

When determining potential synergies in the new paradigm, the analysis must be performed in a holistic, rather than a marginalistic, sense. Customer requirements, market structures, technological systems, and the skills of people determine business systems that actively produce and deliver products and services.

Synergies come from three fundamental sources:

♦ *Buying more from fewer sources*: For example, organizations are under pressure to reduce costs and improve their performance. To do this, they reduce the number of suppliers, hoping to work more efficiently and achieve savings that can be shared.

♦ *Jointly using equipment, resources, and experience*: The systems and resources are leveraged to produce more for less.

♦ *More effectively using administrative or fiduciary resources*: For example, larger corporations have better access to capital markets and can achieve lower capital costs and better cash flow. However, bureaucracies can slow the decision-making process or create the tendency to protect the status quo. When this happens, the result is poor performance.

THE NEW PARADIGM ORGANIZATION: MANAGEMENT AND LEADERSHIP SYSTEMS

Although product/service delivery systems can be stand-alone entities, when synergies can be achieved they can be successfully combined into more complex systems.

Regardless of the new paradigm organization's size, there are only three levels of management/leadership systems, as viewed from the process and system perspective: executive leadership, general management, and operating management.

Executive Leadership System

The executive's responsibilities include creating an inspired vision of the organization's desired future and articulating it in such a way that everyone will be willing to adopt it. An inspired vision drives actions, signals the core values to all stakeholders, and strategically focuses the organization over the long term. A vision clearly defines exactly what the organization stands for and why it merits support.

The mission component of the vision is necessarily of a shorter duration and more specific. The mission and vision together relate to all stakeholders for a term that may extend from three to twenty years.

The senior executives must clearly understand how to manage business components as processes. Major executive processes include generating (or reexamining) a clear vision of the organization's future direction along with processes oriented toward realizing that vision: generating and leading achievement of the mission, strategic planning, and long-term decision making.

When we examine the components that executives consider to be critical to the success of the organization, we find that the least successful organizations are those that focus on results. In contrast, organizations that are the most successful are focused on processes (Figure 6.5).

BUSINESS SYSTEM WITH EXECUTIVE LEADERSHIP SYSTEM

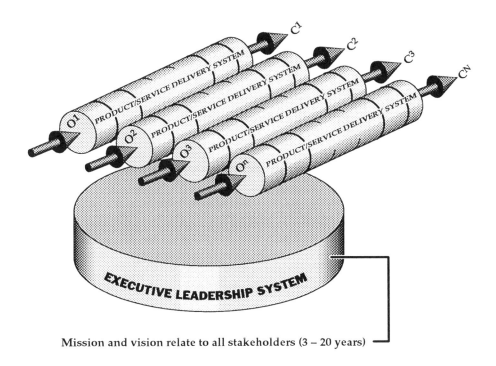

Mission and vision relate to all stakeholders (3 – 20 years)

Figure 6.5

General Management System

The General Management System converts the mission and vision into the broad plans and actions necessary to support the product/service delivery systems. At this level, leaders translate the executive vision into reality through broad strategic initiatives.

The General Management System involves resourcing and coordinating of operations. The focus over a time span of one to three years is on processes such as capital resource allocation, research and development, and human resource utilization. The processes at this level translate the vision and mission into functional and operational terms that enable managers to undertake actions to support the change.

Managers at this level are the front line leaders of paradigm change—the champions of the new system. Their charge to demonstrate the need for change may create the strongest resistance. Their challenge is to exercise active listening skills to defuse resistance while at the same time maintaining a focus on the long-term vision.

In supporting the paradigm change, general management has the responsibility to align the entire organization on value-added processes and avoid the waste of local optimization. This responsibility may extend to identifying reengineering projects and chartering teams to redesign or streamline processes (Figure 6.6).

BUSINESS SYSTEM WITH
GENERAL MANAGEMENT SYSTEM AND
EXECUTIVE LEADERSHIP SYSTEM

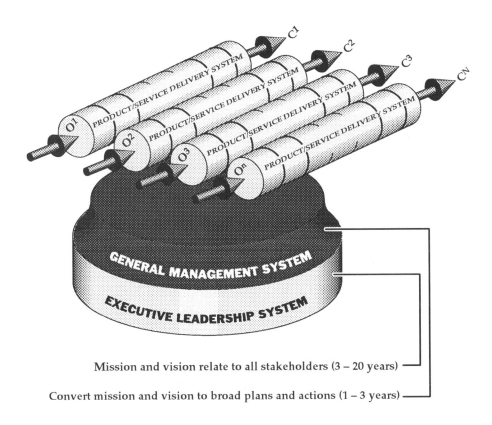

Mission and vision relate to all stakeholders (3 – 20 years)

Convert mission and vision to broad plans and actions (1 – 3 years)

Figure 6.6

Operating Management System

This is the tactical level of the organization. Operating management systems provide direct management support for the product/service delivery systems and focus on a three-month to one-year time frame. Operating management systems include scheduling, maintenance, staffing, and training. Their processes also include the continuous improvement activities aimed at maximizing fixed assets. Establishing an interactive climate for learning and communicating ideas and concerns is paramount for managers and supervisors. Management systems provide the tools and resources. Operating unit managers then empower people to accomplish the mission of their product/service delivery system (Figure 6.7).

The business systems and the executive leadership system are linked to the outside world of customers, vendors, distribution channels, and stakeholders. The general management system and the operating management system are internal links that maintain alignment between the business systems and the executive leadership system. For organizations rooted in the traditional mass-production paradigm, the magnitude and impact of these new paradigm systems cannot be overemphasized.

BUSINESS SYSTEM WITH OPERATING MANAGEMENT SYSTEM, GENERAL MANAGEMENT SYSTEM, AND EXECUTIVE LEADERSHIP SYSTEM

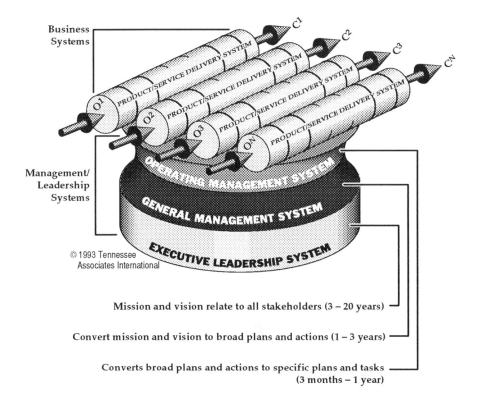

Mission and vision relate to all stakeholders (3 – 20 years)

Convert mission and vision to broad plans and actions (1 – 3 years)

Converts broad plans and actions to specific plans and tasks (3 months – 1 year)

Figure 6.7

LINKING THE
FOUR ORGANIZATIONAL SYSTEMS

Five organizational rivets bind these distinct levels of management and business processes together into an integrated organization (Figure 6.8):

1. Responsibility
2. Accountability
3. Authority/Standards
4. Empowerment
5. Innovation

The entire organization answers in some way to two groups: its customers and its owners. The organization is responsible to its customers, but accountable to its owners.

While being accountable means to be answerable for, being responsible gives power to use available resources to satisfy the customers' wants and needs, subject to any constraints imposed by the owners.

Responsibility flows across the business process to customers.

Accountability, on the other hand, flows from business processes through management processes to owners.

The difference between the two is straightforward—a disappointed customer can choose to patronize a competitor, but a disappointed boss can fire an employee.

THE NEW PARADIGM ORGANIZATION WITH ORGANIZATIONAL RIVETS

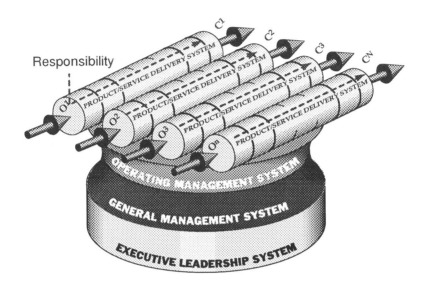

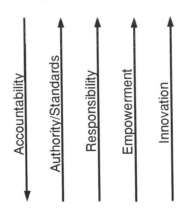

Figure 6.8

Authority is the power to decide the resources over which an individual or team can exercise responsibility. The organization's ability to promote, fire, reward, and discipline are manifestations of power or authority.

Establishing appropriate performance standards is an effective method of exercising authority to align the organization. Standards provide the mechanism for focusing and aligning the organization, and measuring and evaluating performance. Management is responsible for establishing standards and providing guidance and resources for attaining those standards. Furthermore, standards must constantly be monitored and modified to meet market conditions, competitive realities, and exceed customer expectations.

For example, when Federal Express was founded, it established a new standard in the overnight delivery business by promising *next-day delivery* anywhere in the United States. The company was organized so that this standard could be consistently met. Next-day delivery was not the result of a high-technology package-sorting system and aircraft hub in Memphis. On the contrary, Federal Express' standards of next-day delivery dictated that the Memphis infrastructure be built.

New competitors entered the market and Endemic Overcapacity occurred after Federal Express proved that next-day delivery was both possible and profitable. Federal Express then changed the delivery standard from next-day delivery to *by noon the next day.* Processes and systems had to be improved so that this new standard could be met.

Once again, to stay ahead of the competition, the standard was changed from noon to *10:30 a.m., next day.* Processes and systems were changed and investments and improvements made to meet the standard.

As a result of customer research, management determined that further improvements in delivery times would not be worth the cost to meet an earlier standard. In order to add value, two new standards were established. The first was to increase value by *reducing unit cost* so that the organization could be competitively priced. This action denied higher margins to competitors who were trying to stay abreast of the company's advances.

The additional standard involved service enhancement (recall strategies mentioned earlier for coping with Endemic Overcapacity). Added value was attained by tracking packages from pick-up time through delivery. Where non-delivery was claimed, Federal Express was able to identify the recipient and time of receipt.

These new standards gave added strength to the company's marketing efforts. However, even as this is being written, competition is once again rapidly closing the perceived performance gap.

Empowerment is a frequently used but poorly understood term. To empower is to transfer sufficient authority so that individuals or groups can fulfill their responsibilities. In business processes, people are empowered to fulfill the organization's responsibility to the customer. In all internal processes, people are empowered to fulfill the responsibility to the entity that receives the output of their process.

However, experience demonstrates that empowered people, when intimately involved in a process, are usually psychologically unwilling or unable to declare that process obsolete. They typically resist the introduction of new and different processes or systems.

Innovation is the process of creating something so new and different that it renders obsolete comparable processes, products, or services. All processes, products, and services are subject to the pressures of competitive improvements and innovation. To gain and maintain a competitive position, innovation must have a high priority. Although the idea of innovation is usually associated with profound change, a relatively small improvement can result in a major breakthrough.

The following illustration of the S-curve of the life cycle shows how the ability of a product, process, or service to contribute approaches zero over time (Figure 6.9).

S-CURVE

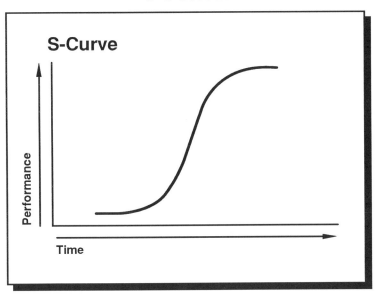

Figure 6.9

When the top of the "S" is reached, innovation is required to restore margin and competitive position. To predict the development of the S-curve in products or services, it is critical to monitor price, profit, sales, and market share. The S-curve in processes can be determined by monitoring issues such as cost, cycle time, safety, and quality.

Leadership is responsible for creating the management processes and systems designed to look for new and better processes and systems. Leaders must also follow through to ensure that the organization adopts these new technologies or processes. The challenge facing leaders is to get the organization to think about process innovation on an on-going basis so that opportunities can be seized. Theoretically, the right time to innovate would be when market acceptance and competitive conditions yield the greatest return on investment. Innovations too far in advance may not be accepted by the market. Innovations made too late will find the market lost to competition. Since the precise point in time for innovation to be most effective cannot be determined, leaders must rely on three pathways to innovation:

♦ *Continuous improvement.* Innovation occurs as a natural output of well-managed continuous process improvement. It is analogous to going to bat to get a base hit and hitting a home run instead.

♦ *Random improvement.* Innovation occurs most often when teams get together to discuss customer feedback, brainstorm possibilities, or simply to ask "why not."

♦ *Specific management direction (reengineering).* Innovation is planned by management in a specific area using allocated resources. Unfortunately, this reactive attempt to manage the S-curve often occurs when the organization's competitive position has seriously deteriorated.

The ultimate accountability for innovation belongs to the most senior management team. Leaders must assure that the culture of the company encourages:

- Open questioning of why and how
- Open discussion
- Positive attitudes
- A feeling of security from negative consequences (for example, innovating oneself out of a job)
- Search for the new instead of comfort with the status quo
- An understanding of change and the dynamics of change

CHAPTER 7

THE HIGH PERFORMANCE LEADER

The best leader is the one who has sense enough to pick good people...and the self-restraint to keep from meddling with them...

– Theodore Roosevelt

There is a tendency to view managers as administrators of the status quo who are emotionally detached from their work. In contrast, leaders are viewed as innovators who introduce new approaches and achieve excitement through their work.

Some see the distinction as between tasks: leadership involves coping with change; management involves coping with complexity. Leadership is leading change, not being led by change.

The qualities of good leaders and good managers are not mutually exclusive, but mutually supportive. Every successful executive must have:

* The visionary mind of the leader to create change
* The administrative mind of the manager to cope with complexity

The more senior the rank, the more necessary are leadership skills. The ultimate success of the organization is dependent on the inspiration and leadership of the senior executive at the highest level.

In our early work with a company recognized today for its high level of quality and productivity, we found a significant example of the importance of leadership. After completing training of operating managers of several facilities, we visited their organizations for on-site coaching. Significant results were observed only where the senior site executive had taken an active leadership role in the improvement process. Without direction and support from their leaders, other well-intentioned and properly trained managers were floundering.

VISION

Visions are the vehicles that transport us across the boundaries of current reality to the boundless hopes of a future seemingly beyond our grasp. What once we deemed impossible becomes not only possible but probable when we live out our vision through our actions.

—Fred L. Smith
Chief Executive Officer
Tennessee Associates International

Leadership is the ability to create and articulate a vision of the future state of the organization with such clarity and vigor that the members embrace and implement that vision as their own. Leadership is a dynamic process because it provides the basic energy to initiate the actions that create an organization-wide commitment to high performance.

The senior management team has responsibility for facilitating the development of the organization's vision in a way that assures enthusiastic acceptance by all members. The process of creating the vision is as important as the vision statement itself. The vision statement is a concise written description that evokes a compelling image of the organization's future.

The vision statement has four components:

1. *The fundamental purpose of the organization in timeless, broadly defined words.* When Steve Jobs was at Apple he stated the vision as, "To make a contribution to the world by making tools for the mind that advance humankind."[1] That statement evokes an image of the future around which managers can set both short-term and long-term goals.

2. *A mission stated as a specific long-term goal.* In 1961, President Kennedy stated NASA's mission as "achieving the goal, before this decade is out, of landing a man on the Moon and returning him safely to Earth." This was certainly a clear statement of "what" and "when."[2]

3. *A vivid image of the organization's desired future.*
When Yamaha articulated its objective to become
number one in the Japanese motorcycle industry,
Honda proclaimed a vivid new image: "Yamaha wo
tsubusu!" This translates roughly as, "We will crush,
squash, slaughter Yamaha!"[3] Then Honda put its new
vivid image into action by accelerating new product
introduction—averaging more than one new product
per week during the next year.

4. *A set of guiding values or principles that tells how the
organization operates in attaining the desired future.*
Guiding values consist of general principles or ide-
als, such as honesty or fairness, that guide action.
An organization's guiding values indicate priorities
in conducting relationships with all customers and
stakeholders.

Only the organization's leaders can initiate and promote
the development of a vision that the entire organization will
embrace. I have never met a senior executive who did not
think he or she had a clear vision. Too often, that "clear
vision" was shared with only a few other people. The vision
must tell everyone "where we are going" and "what we will
become." Ideally, the vision enthuses and inspires as it
speaks to people's hearts, as well as to their heads. The
vision is expressed through strategic initiatives. When

actions are not taken to implement visions, the visions are not fulfilled.

The first time Tennessee Associates met with Vaughn Beals, CEO of Harley-Davidson, the company was in serious danger of going out of business. In that meeting, it was evident that Beals had a clear vision of where he wanted to go and how he expected to get there. As we began to help implement that vision, we had no idea that Harley-Davidson would one day be recognized as a classic corporate turn-around. When Beals shared his vision with us and his senior management team, we clearly understood what needed to be accomplished. That shared vision guided Harley-Davidson to success.

Senior leaders cannot delegate their leadership responsibility. The risks are too great. Senior executives must demonstrate their leadership by taking the initiative in articulating clear vision and sound values. The creation of a consistent and firm vision and core beliefs allows the structure to be flexible so people can focus on rapid implementation of the strategic initiatives. The diagram on the following page illustrates that the broadly defined vision interacts with both the guiding values and the more definitive mission to propel the organization to the successful desired future (Figure 7.1).

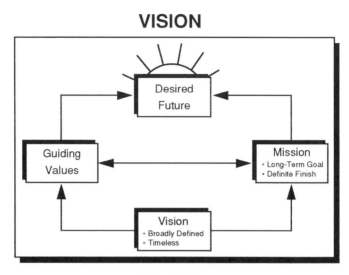

Figure 7.1

In a study it was determined that major companies described as having a vision performed considerably better than those that did not. In searching for the underlying reason that explained the better performance, it was decided that visionary companies have clearly articulated core values and a mission. Both result from the vision.

The fundamental objective in the process of developing a vision statement is to force people to think differently and to understand a new paradigm. Vision, values, and mission cannot easily be separated from one another and are often blended into the organization's identity statement. When developed by a consensus process and articulated in a compelling way by leaders, the identity statement becomes a powerful unifying force for the organization. An effective statement evokes a shared vision of what the organization is trying to do and becomes the guiding principle that remains constant in the progress toward the future.

HARD DECISIONS

High performance leaders look for information to help them make decisions. Every decision cannot be made with empirical data. Deming asked, "who can measure the cost of a lost customer?" The fact that accurate measurement can be difficult in some circumstances is reason enough to consider the implications of these "unmeasurables."

American Express measures scrap and re-work in its marketing and customer information programs using the term "avoidable input." Customer inquiries are examined to determine cause—such as clarification of an advertising campaign or a billing statement. If the advertisements or billing had been clear, the inquiries would have been "avoidable." When a customer requests additional information, the communication process is essentially being re-worked, and the initial communication to inform the customer can be considered scrap.

In Norman Dixon's extensive study[4] of the success and failure of British military leadership, he cites the following reasons for leadership failure:

- *Anxiety* has a crippling effect on perception, memory, and thought.
- A *fundamental conservatism and clinging to outworn tradition*—in other words, an inability to get out of old paradigm thinking.
- A *tendency to reject or ignore information*—the greater the impact of new information, the more strenuously it is resisted.

A common thread among the reasons for leadership failure is the resistance to new information that might change the course of action. Dr. Laurence J. Peter championed the idea of the Peter Principle, which is: "In a hierarchy, every employee tends to rise to his level of incompetence."[5] The common characteristic of incompetence is not that good people are promoted until they reach the level of incompetence; rather it is that they reached the heights by functioning a certain way, and continue to function the same way, regardless of major changes in the world around them. That is how good junior executives can become bad senior executives. They do what they know.

In High Performance Organizations, people are not told how to do their jobs on the basis of one person's perceptions. Actions taken are informed responses to organized information. Data-based decisions require more time, but they also have a much greater probability of being right.

Too often, senior leaders are overloaded with data, but have little meaningful information about what is really happening. A computer will signal when it is overloaded; the human mind has no such mechanism. Most often the best solution is to push decision making down to properly trained and empowered people at the lowest level.

High performance leaders also recognize they will never have enough information to make decisions. When swift action is required, the leader must exercise his or her own judgment and make that great "mental leap in the dark."

THE DRIVING FORCE

As the driving force of the new paradigm organization, leadership calls for new directions that will lead to improved performance and greater customer satisfaction. In every area, performance must improve at a rate that stays ahead of ever-increasing customer expectations and competition.

One of America's great military leaders, General George Patton, was a firm believer in the right kind of leadership. Warren J. Ridge describes Patton's management philosophy: "Productivity problems were not high on his daily agenda. He figured that if a leader planned well, motivated, promoted teamwork, created high morale, and made sure people knew what they were supposed to do and why, productivity [and output] would result automatically."[6]

Alignment Throughout
The Organization

At every level, leaders are accountable for understanding and supporting organizational vision and mission as well as their own. They must ensure that their area of responsibility is aligned with the central purpose of the organization.

A vacuum in leadership cannot exist if the organization is to achieve high performance. In the absence of sound senior leadership, competing visions will emerge. For example, marketing and production will compete to provide their own focus and achieve local optimization. Conflicting values will emerge and legitimate structures will be undermined as the power struggle increases. The resulting destructive energy will divide rather than unify the organization. The customer is forgotten in the political battle.

Organizations that decide to be aligned with the customer are structured to allow people to "get close to the customer." All business processes are aligned with the customer's requirements, and all management processes are organized to support a customer focus.

When strategy has been determined, key processes throughout the organization must be aligned to support the strategy. This is accomplished through interaction between leaders and process owners by reconciling team missions and processes so that all accept responsibility for achieving their goals. Leaders must align the systems and structures to encourage people to perform to the maximum of their ability, and then support with training that can increase the ability and expand the performance.

To facilitate alignment, each leader must reconcile the organization's broad goals with each team's specific goals. This requires interaction between leaders and their teams. Commitment and alignment grow out of open dialogue in a consensus-oriented environment. Leaders must understand the team's reservations and use that information to shape implementation of the mission. By allocating resources to activities that support the mission, leaders can break down barriers and guide the organization into the future.

ESTABLISH STANDARDS

Clear standards provide the methodology for expressing performance expectations and measuring compliance. When standards are established and clearly communicated, management has the means for maintaining process performance consistently.

General H. Norman Schwarzkopf writes about his service under General Latham in Alaska, "[The General] also set me and my staff to work writing standards for our commanders. By summer, we had a single sheet of paper for each type of platoon that spelled out the skills we expected that unit to master. . .I could hand that paper to the platoon leader and tell him, 'This is how I will measure your unit's performance. I will never grade you on anything that is not on this sheet.' Meanwhile, Latham promulgated individual standards for fitness in Arctic and mountaineering skills. His lists enabled us to focus our preparations in a way I'd never imagined possible."[7]

DEFINE BOUNDARIES

Effective teamwork starts with a good procedure for writing team charters to accomplish specific objectives in support of the strategic initiatives. Teams are either permanent or temporary. Permanent teams are organized around natural processes. Temporary teams are organized across functions or processes and chartered to achieve improvements in a specific part of the process flow.

The energies of human potential are released through the decentralization and clearly defined delegation of responsibility and authority. In the words of Luis Suarez, President of Pepsi-Cola, Latin America, "Empowerment without accountability is like giving a loaded pistol to a monkey." The results can be devastating for all concerned.

Senior management should not cut itself off from processes in order to manage strategy and finances. Senior management must make sure it manages only its own processes. Authority to manage a process must be delegated to those closest to the process.

ALLOCATE RESOURCES

One of the most critical responsibilities of leaders is providing and allocating the resources required for the organization to fulfill its mission. The decision of what resources to allocate and where to allocate them is "where the rubber meets the road" in implementation.

In the old paradigm, managers maintained maximum control. In the new paradigm, leaders delegate maximum control. It is the leader's job to provide the training, resources, and structures that enable people to perform at the highest possible levels. Rather than instructing people in what management perceives as a remedy, training and resources must be allocated to people who have been empowered to solve problems. The involvement of people is crucial and leads to self-fulfillment that achieves results exceeding expectations.

LEADERS' RESPONSIBILITY FOR CHANGE

How can leaders manage change when the biggest change that may be needed is in the way the leaders themselves manage? If we want to change others, we must first change ourselves. The more radical the desired change, the more radically the leaders must change.

The most frequent change posture I see adopted by senior executives is to delegate someone to examine the latest management fad. The more time subordinates spend examining the current fad, the more likely they are to recommend it as the solution. Not to recommend that which has been so thoroughly investigated would confirm that time had been wasted and would leave the chief investigator without a project to lead. The key issue in these decisions to adopt the latest fad is that the investigator's recommendation does not have to be right—it just cannot be wrong. While the fad is gaining steam, any recommendation not to follow the crowd would, of course, seem wrong—and the Hawthorne experiments prove there is always some benefit from change. However, the change to the new paradigm is more fundamental. It requires refocusing the vision and mission. It also requires leadership involvement in implementing major changes in the structure and culture.

Too often, people have told us of management-instituted programs that paid only lip service to achieving change—no wonder they failed. High Performance Organizations don't result from "read my lips" sermons, they only result from "watch my feet" leadership. If the people in the organization are not convinced that management is committed to the High Performance Organization, nothing happens.

Successful change is usually initiated from the top down, not from the bottom up. Lower-level initiative is fine, but it will not be sustained without total commitment by the senior executive and his or her team. The senior executive's role is to create the structures and systems that enable them to lead dramatic changes in the very fiber of their organization. They own the keys to the methodology that shapes the culture. The willingness to change and the tenacity to follow through are qualities perhaps best exemplified by the original founders of great business organizations.

The new paradigm leader believes that people want to be productive and make a real contribution. Andrew A. DuBrin, a leading psychologist, points out that the need to be productive and efficient is a necessary ingredient of self-esteem. Surveys indicate that what matters most about a job is not money, but the self-fulfillment of making a contribution—a sense of accomplishment and achievement.

The point is that our beliefs about people have a profound impact on our actions. When we expect a certain behavior of people and set up a system based on these expectations, the system will ensure that the expected behaviors are manifested. Systems based on the expectation that people want to contribute result in improved performance. Low expectations produce poor results; high expectations produce high results.

CREATING AND MAINTAINING CULTURE

Culture can be the greatest roadblock or the best facilitator in the transition to high performance. The new paradigm culture enables the organization to focus on critical issues and react quickly to change. The knowledge of results is only a measure of past performance. What is critical is being organized to anticipate, or at least react to, future events.

When the Japanese emerged as a productive world force, many believed their productivity was a result of a different cultural heritage. That myth was dispelled when Japanese management systems and American workers dramatically increased productivity at newly acquired plants in America.

It is not culture at the national level that makes the difference, but culture at the corporate level. With the right kind of corporate culture, members of any national culture can produce top-quality work. The shape of an organization's culture is the CEO's responsibility.

Changes in cultural values must be communicated and practiced by management. One of Tennessee Associates' instructors tells about the senior staff meeting in his former organization where the decision was made that male managers need not wear ties at work. When he communicated the information to his staff, he was wearing a tie and so were all the men of his staff. All week he wore a tie; so did they. The next Monday he came to work without a tie and by noon all of his staff had taken off their ties.

Speeches, posters, and balloons in the atrium are not the answer. In order to overcome the inertia of the existing culture, the new culture must manifest itself in every action of senior managers. Employees are less convinced by what management is saying than by what they see management doing. Only actions have real credibility. The leaders must truly "walk the talk."

LEADERS AS FOLLOWERS

Good leaders must be good followers who are forthright and honest in providing feedback to the organization. They are sincerely committed to alignment with the organization as a whole. Good followers are accountable for their own actions and performance. They will not be caught in the psychological trap of denial of their failures and shortcomings. This denial inhibits the ability to make changes necessary for personal growth and improvement, or results in projection of the blame for personal failure on others.

Good followers are also good learners, and the higher a person's rank, the more important it is that he or she learn.

SET A PERSONAL EXAMPLE

Research indicates that leadership style has a powerful impact on organizational unity and team effectiveness. Leaders must set personal examples clearly and remain steadfastly consistent.

They must adopt a style of leadership that facilitates the communication, consensus, and empowerment that encourages change. The ideal leader understands that people, rather than techniques, are what really matter. The high performance leader "leads," in every sense of the word, toward achievement of personal and organizational excellence. The leader's values serve as the glue that holds the structure together and signals "who we are" and "what we believe." Implementing the values is an expression of the leader's commitment.

When things are not going well, leadership needs to exude a sense of confidence. When things are going well, leaders need to focus on anticipating the future needs.

The leader must visibly practice teamwork. He or she must actively use teamwork tools at every opportunity. This action endorses and promotes the validity of team concepts.

The person who really needs to be convinced of the viability of the High Performance Organization is the organization's leader—the chief executive officer. Using the authority this position commands, the CEO can set in motion a chain of events that will transform the entire corporation. Under enlightened leadership, changes will be cascaded through the organization. Effecting this change and making it work requires a leadership style dramatically different from that of the old paradigm.

CHAPTER 8

IT IS TIME TO PLAN AND ACT

It is no use saying, "we are doing our best." You have got to succeed in doing what is necessary.

—**Winston Churchill**

The belief that knowledge is power shapes our ideas about who has more potential for a job. We tend to judge a person's intelligence by his or her ability to process and store information.

When asked to compare the performance of American managers to that of German managers, a famous management consultant's tongue-in-cheek response was that the German manager was evaluated based on the weight of the briefcase he carried home, while the American manager was evaluated based on how bright he was. The audience of American managers beamed with pleasure at what they thought was a compliment, until he added "and I don't know which is worse." His point was that performance should be the criteria—not the amount of activity the manager engages in or how bright he or she is. We should modify the cliché that knowledge is power to "power is the ability to effectively apply knowledge."

A plan of action for change is required to create a High Performance Organization. The level of success is determined by the ability of the people who must lead and direct the change.

Change for the sake of change is a major source of organizational frustration and waste. First, we must ask the most basic question of all:

+ Does my organization need to change?

If we objectively determine that change is necessary, the remaining questions to be answered are:

+ What kind of changes are required?
+ How will these changes be implemented?

DOES MY ORGANIZATION NEED TO CHANGE?

There are a series of logical steps needed to develop a ration-al response to the fundamental question, "Does my organization need to change?" These are illustrated in the flow chart on the facing page (Figure 8.1).

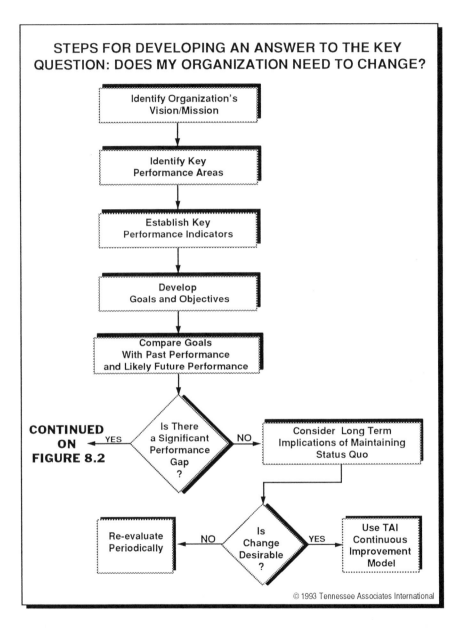

Figure 8.1

157

The first step is to identify the organization's vision and mission. Looking at a corporation as a whole, its vision and mission should drive the analysis. When considering one component of a larger organization:

- ▲ If the vision and mission already exist, make sure they have meaning and are relevant to the overall vision and mission.
- ▲ If there is no vision and mission, create clear, crisp, concise vision and mission statements. Although not always an easy task, this foundation is imperative.

The next step is to identify the key areas of performance that will be essential to performing the mission within the parameters of the vision. Proper organizational alignment can be attained only when the day-to-day tasks are consistent with the big picture. When the day-to-day components take on a meaning that is inconsistent with the vision and mission, performance suffers.

After identifying key performance areas, you will find the only meaningful way to assess the organization's performance is to establish relevant indicators and measures. These indicators and measures tell us about the organization by tracking customer satisfaction, market performance, competitive capabilities, financial flow, and innovation. They can help determine when change is required and provide a viable base for gauging future performance. To achieve maximum benefits, predictions should be judged against relevant goals and objectives that are continuously examined for applicability and accuracy.

Next, compare projections of the key performance measures with goals and objectives. Then determine if there are any significant gaps between goals and objectives and predictions of future performance. If there are significant gaps, determine what kind of change is required.

If there are no major gaps, examine the other forces that affect the organization. Even if change is not necessary now, the chaos in today's markets and the prevalence of Endemic Overcapacity demand that managers and leaders examine the issue of change.

Installing a continuous improvement system driven by process management will dramatically benefit any organization. The amount and speed of change necessary can be designed and planned according to the characteristics of the organization, its resources, competitive pressures, customer expectations, and performance requirements.

WHAT KIND OF CHANGE IS REQUIRED?

In organizations that have identified significant performance gaps, a series of evaluations must be made in order to determine the necessary changes. First, analyze the gaps to determine root causes of shortfalls. It is critical to determine whether our current strategies are appropriate, or are the cause of the performance gaps we have identified (Figure 8.2). If the existing strategies are not appropriate, the next logical step is to develop new strategies or modify existing ones.

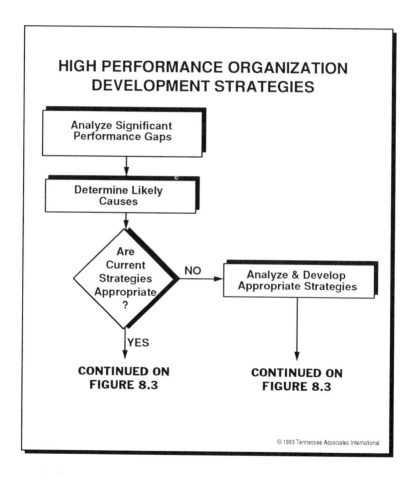

Figure 8.2

When satisfied that strategies are appropriate, move to the next critical decision: are the organization's culture and structures compatible with strategies? (Figure 8.3) Since appropriate strategies are determined by market trends and conditions, structure must follow the strategies, rather than letting the structure limit strategies.

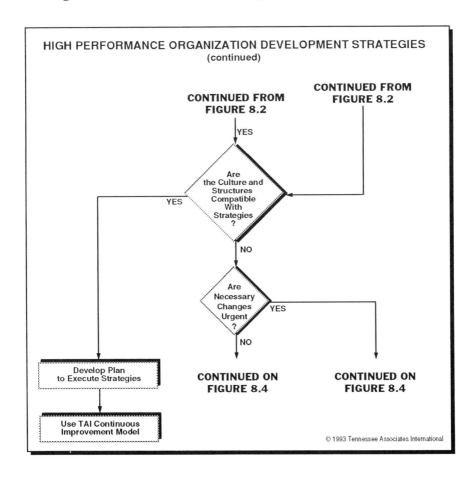

Figure 8.3

The High Performance Organization's structures and systems are based on processes. Make sure that the organization is thoroughly process-oriented and structured around relevant processes.

If relatively minor modifications are required, major structural or cultural transformation is not necessary. In that case, we can rely on a continuous improvement model reinforced with process management to help close the gaps.

If the culture and structure of the organization must be significantly changed, then determine what kind of changes are required. How urgent is the situation? Must these changes be made quickly? (Figure 8.4)

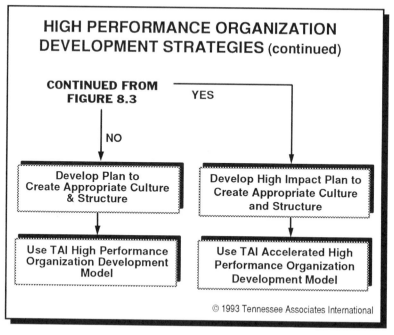

Figure 8.4

Unfortunately, one of the implications of Endemic Over-capacity and chaos is that by the time organizations discover they must change, they must do so with urgency.

How Will the Changes be Implemented?

Because every organization is unique, each needs to develop its own plan to implement organizational changes. Over the years, Tennessee Associates International has developed several fundamental models to guide the planning and implementation processes:

♦ Continuous Improvement Model—evolutionary changes toward high performance, no structural transformation required
♦ Structural Transformation Model—to achieve high performance, both structural and cultural transformation are required
♦ Greenfield Model—high performance for new organizations

All models provide a system to help managers plan and implement change.

The Continuous Improvement Model
A Management System Based on
Process Management

Even if we do not intend to drastically change the structure of the organization, a plan for the successful introduction of a system of process-management-based continuous improvement is required. The key to success is to focus on managing processes instead of on isolated activities and results. Leaders must be willing to modify the organizational structure to meet the requirements of processes and systems.

The first phase of the Continuous Improvement Model requires the development of understanding and commitment among senior managers to drive their active leadership of the implementation process. In fact, the entire first phase of planning and implementation belongs to the top management team, which is composed of the most senior manager and his or her direct reports. This senior team is called the steering team. They "own" the implementation process.

Since the steering team (top management group) is responsible for implementing the new management system, members must learn how to function as an effective team in order to set the right example. The purpose of the first phase of the Continuous Improvement Model is for the team to evaluate the organization and ensure that the various management and process teams are properly identified and aligned with the organization's strategies. Using this information, the steering team must develop an appropriate implementation model and plan for the new management system. Within the relatively evolutionary world of this general model, the plan must reflect the realities of time and other pressures on the organization's need to change.

With the broad pattern of a plan as a guideline, the steering team must identify specific implementation requirements and allocate the necessary resources. The implementation plan should include two other critical components.

The first is an effective plan to communicate the new management system to all stakeholders. The second is a set of measures for tracking the implementation process to assure that the organization continues to satisfy its customers and meet its performance targets. To manage the implementation process, we must be able to measure it and be willing to intervene when improvements must be made. Measures of both implementation and organizational performance are crucial to an effective and successful implementation effort.

After the plan is finalized, the steering team launches the next phase, which cascades a system of process management through established team structures. All groups responsible and accountable for managing processes must practice effective teamwork. Throughout this phase of the Continuous Improvement Model, management teams use process management to identify, catalog, and manage the significant processes and systems that support the organization's mission and strategies. The role of the steering team, and every natural management team, is to lead by example, manage their processes as a team, provide ongoing training and support, communicate process improvement results, and constantly recognize and reinforce good efforts of everyone involved in the implementation process.

The next phase continues the transition to a process-management-based continuous improvement system. The natural management teams employ a process management methodology that encompasses critical processes at all levels. Simultaneously, the necessary support systems are developed and deployed, including: obtaining and utilizing the voice of the customer, rewarding and recognizing performance, documenting processes, benchmarking, partnering with customers and suppliers, and innovating.

When these steps are successfully completed, the organization's culture, structure, and systems are dedicated to the attainment of customer satisfaction and organizational excellence. Throughout the implementation process, the steering team must measure, evaluate, and intervene in order to successfully attain a state where strategies are aligned through processes focused on organizational performance and customer satisfaction.

Structural Transformation Model Creating the High Performance Organization

The ultimate goal of the Structural Transformation Model is to create a High Performance Organization. This high performance model provides a framework within which special solutions are developed for special conditions and general solutions are developed for general conditions. The purpose of this model is to help plan and implement a process to convert an organization from a management system based on the traditional paradigm to one based on the high performance paradigm.

When applying the Structural Transformation Model, expect to effect major structural and cultural transformation at the outset of the implementation process. In this process, some of today's players may no longer be required in the resulting organization. Careful consideration will need to be given to how personnel changes are made.

After the decision has been made to use the Structural Transformation Model to achieve high performance, there are three specific stages of implementation:

- Planning and Designing
- Preparing to Launch The New Management System
- Launching the High Performance Organization

167

Planning and Designing

To effectively cope with these conditions, the senior manager must create and charter a change management team composed of qualified senior personnel who will remain with the organization after the transformation is completed. The change management team creates and charters the appropriate design team(s) to perform the staff and support functions required by the planning process. The line leadership role is performed by the change management team, which includes the most senior manager. The change management team is responsible for the entire process.

The principle steps for the designing and planning phase are listed in the flowchart in the left column of Figure 8.5. The design team should include at least one person from the change management team, and that person should be the design team leader. The design team tasks are listed in the right column. The broad arrow between the two columns represents the need to continuously reconcile the steps within and between both columns. It is not a step-by-step process as it appears on paper—each individual activity affects all the others. These teams are engaged in a dynamic and interactive process.

At the tip of the arrow in the center of Figure 8.5 we see the need to develop appropriate measures to help monitor the organization's performance and the implementation process.

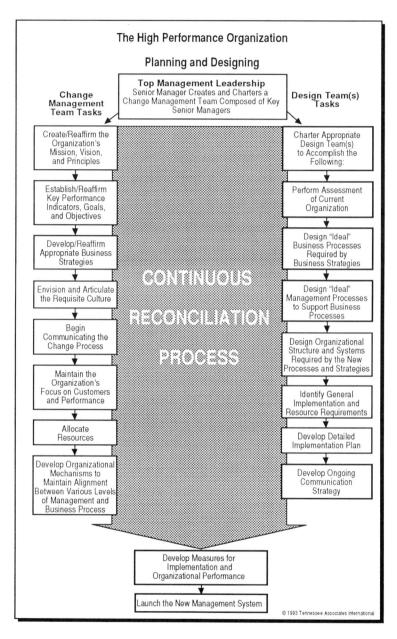

Figure 8.5

Preparing to Launch the New Management System

When the tasks in the Planning and Design Phase are completed, the change management team is ready to transfer its attention to the next phase: Preparing to Launch the New Management System (Figure 8.6). The change management team's tasks are on the left; the design team's are on the right. All tasks are conducted in an atmosphere of continuous reconciliation.

The steps in the figures in this chapter are logical and straightforward; however, clarity is not synonymous with triviality. Each step is important and requires a great deal of thinking, soul-searching, and planning before it can be completed. The required changes will have a tremendous impact, both positive and negative, on individuals and their families. These issues do not mitigate against change, but they do demand careful analysis, planning, and execution so that the organization and its associates are properly served.

Again, as in the Planning and Design Phase, all tasks are conducted in an atmosphere of continuous reconciliation. The systems chosen for implementation must be fully aligned with the business strategies. The business strategies must be continuously evaluated and modified based on feedback related to the systems' success and to the organization's performance.

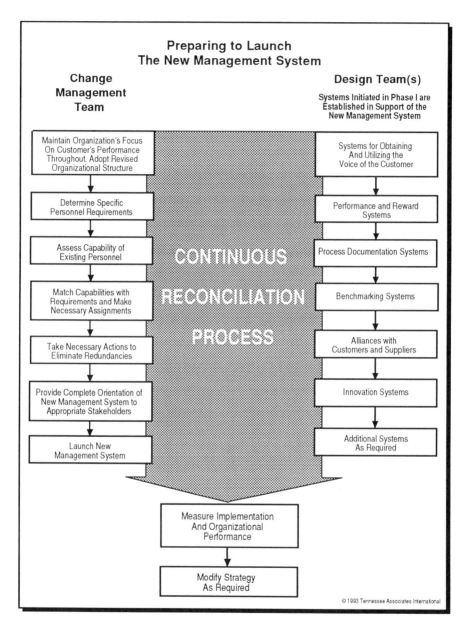

**Preparing to Launch
The New Management System**

**Change
Management
Team**

Design Team(s)
Systems Initiated in Phase I are
Established in Support of the
New Management System

Maintain Organization's Focus On Customer's Performance Throughout. Adopt Revised Organizational Structure	Systems for Obtaining And Utilizing the Voice of the Customer
Determine Specific Personnel Requirements	Performance and Reward Systems
Assess Capability of Existing Personnel	Process Documentation Systems
Match Capabilities with Requirements and Make Necessary Assignments	Benchmarking Systems
Take Necessary Actions to Eliminate Redundancies	Alliances with Customers and Suppliers
Provide Complete Orientation of New Management System to Appropriate Stakeholders	Innovation Systems
Launch New Management System	Additional Systems As Required

CONTINUOUS
RECONCILIATION
PROCESS

Measure Implementation
And Organizational
Performance

Modify Strategy
As Required

© 1993 Tennessee Associates International

Figure 8.6

171

Launching the High Performance Organization

Once the new structure is in place, we can launch the new management system and begin managing processes throughout the organization (Figure 8.7). When the strategy is correct and the culture and structure are aligned, the organization can simultaneously focus on customer satisfaction and performance in a much more optimal way than could be achieved with the traditional management paradigm.

Sustaining the High Performance Organization depends upon the implementation and practice of process management to its fullest extent. The Launch Phase is absolutely critical to any successful transformation to high performance.

The activities to this point have been primarily planning and designing. Now it is time to put the new organization into action. This will require significant training in team skills and process management methodology. Only when the entire organization has fully implemented this phase can the organization be considered to have attained the status of high performance.

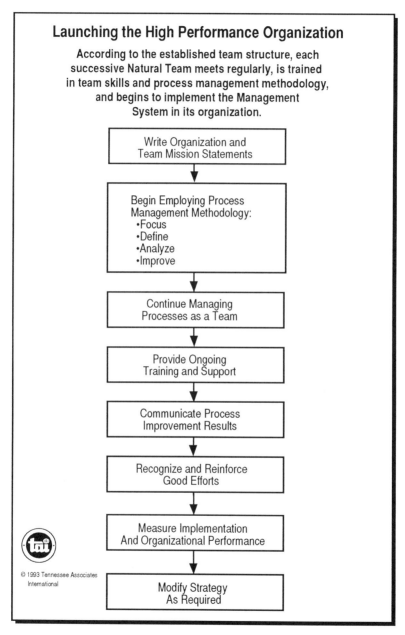

Launching the High Performance Organization

According to the established team structure, each successive Natural Team meets regularly, is trained in team skills and process management methodology, and begins to implement the Management System in its organization.

Write Organization and Team Mission Statements

Begin Employing Process Management Methodology:
•Focus
•Define
•Analyze
•Improve

Continue Managing Processes as a Team

Provide Ongoing Training and Support

Communicate Process Improvement Results

Recognize and Reinforce Good Efforts

Measure Implementation And Organizational Performance

© 1993 Tennessee Associates International

Modify Strategy As Required

Figure 8.7

173

The Urgency Factor

We have presented and described the model that serves as a guide for designing, planning, preparing, and launching a paradigm shift in a functioning organization. An organization does not typically enjoy the luxury of stopping operations, carefully planning changes, testing the plan, and then relaunching operations after the changes have been implemented. It is like the pit stop at a race track where all maintenance and replacement must be achieved in a manner that does not impede victory. Customers must be served, stakeholders must be satisfied, and payroll must be met throughout the change process.

It is extremely important to begin promptly and move rapidly. The shorter the decision time, the sooner the decision can be communicated, allowing everyone to proceed more rapidly to the execution of the task. This reduces the length of the disruption and increases the possibility of successful execution.

When the need to change is urgent, time becomes one of the most, if not the most, critical factors. The relationship between the force it will take and the time available to overcome the barriers to change involves the interaction of resources, focus, priority, and the willingness to apply organizational power.

The illustration on the next page shows that the shorter the time, the more force must be applied (Figure 8.8a).

CHANGE: TIME VS. FORCE

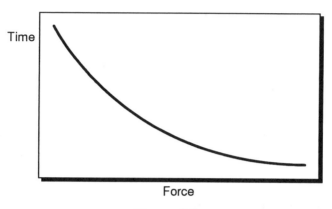

Figure 8.8a

A second critical factor is the magnitude of change and the amount of required fundamental change in culture. The next illustration shows that as the magnitude of change increases, additional force is required (Figure 8.8b).

CHANGE: MAGNITUDE VS. FORCE

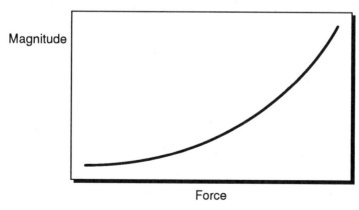

Figure 8.8b

The order in which steps are executed and the amount of care and caution that goes into each step varies according to circumstances. In planning for and implementing change, there is the risk that we will make a mistake, as well as the risk of moving too slowly and too cautiously. The trade-offs and consequences must be evaluated by the change management team, and then the design and implementation plan and process must be handled accordingly. Well-focused plans implemented rapidly will usually be more successful than plans implemented at a slower pace.

THE PERFORMANCE TURNAROUND AT HARLEY-DAVIDSON

The success of the turnaround at Harley-Davidson serves as an excellent example of planning and implementing change to achieve high performance. Founded in 1903, Harley-Davidson is one of the oldest manufacturing companies in the United States.

The American motorcycle industry has moved in and out of conditions of Endemic Overcapacity created by both domestic and foreign producers. At one time over 200 motorcycle producers existed in the U.S.A. By 1953 Harley-Davidson was the only remaining American manufacturer.

The company—privately held for many years—went public in 1965 and merged with AMF in 1969. Ten years later, AMF changed strategic direction from a mix of 2/3 leisure products and 1/3 industrial to a 50/50 mix. When this transition quickly translated into constrained investment, Harley's top managers suggested that AMF divest the company. A buyout was arranged and Harley-Davidson returned to private ownership.

Production was trebled in the first four years of AMF ownership, leading to catastrophic quality problems. Combined with out-of-date designs and high prices, Harley-Davidson was extremely vulnerable to Japan's fresh designs, high quality, and low prices. Despite these problems, the momentum of a rapidly expanding market at the time of the buyout permitted Harley to enjoy record profits and to get a good start on product redesign and quality improvements.

However, the serious recession, high interest rates, and President Carter's credit restrictions resulted in a 20% decline in the heavyweight motorcycle market. That, plus a flood of imported Harley look-alikes and a crushing debt load, caused Harley's market share to drop to 23% (from 90% ten years before). As well, the company lost money for the first time in 50 years—forcing it to even further increase its debt load.

The visionary, disciplined management team, under the leadership of Vaughn Beals, began to build a performance recovery. Internally, major changes were implemented in the following areas.

- *Product line.* Beals says, "What worked was a careful return to early designs. Very simply, we've tried to make current products look like the models of the '40s and '50s—with carefully disguised contemporary technology. Our biggest success has been the Softail and Springer designs that exploit very advanced engineering designs and materials to achieve new products that replicate old models."
- *Employee involvement.* Improved employee participation started with quality circles in the late '70s. Employee involvement eventually became a way of life as people were trained and empowered as process owners.
- *JIT (Just-In-Time).* By shrinking inventory and providing material as needed, JIT reduced the purchase debt.
- *SQC (Statistical Quality Control).* SQC was implemented because JIT became impractical without improved quality. However, the improved quality had far-reaching effects beyond the original need of helping JIT reduce costs.

In 1983, CEO Beals shared with Tennessee Associates his desire to achieve a turnaround in performance and requested our assistance. Of course, no one had to tell the corporate executive committee they were responsible and accountable for survival and growth.

Over time, the focus on high performance drove all aspects of the business. The successful result is a well-known testimony to a leadership focused on both performance and Harley-Davidson's soundest business assets—well-established dealer network and an extraordinarily loyal customer base.

Here are some of the principles underlying the customer focus and performance excellence that made the Harley-Davidson turnaround successful:

+ *Define your niche and stick to it.* Harley concentrated all its resources on one segment of the market. Today, it has a dominant share of the high-end market.
+ *Listen to your customers and give them what they want.* Harley sought feedback from its customers, and then evaluated and used that input. The customer input drove appropriate process changes.
+ *Develop strong points of differentiation.* The marketing differentiation at Harley extended beyond the product. The Harley Owner's Group was a key factor in making customer focus a viable part of Harley's strategy.
+ *Compete on value, not on price.* Harley-Davidson established its competitive edge on the overall value to the customer.

- *Partner with your distribution channel.* Harley appreciated that its loyal dealers were solid assets. Further investments in helping dealers paid off.
- *Build on your name.* The licensing program was used as a two-edged sword. Offensively, licensed products helped build brand recognition and strengthened dealer floor traffic. Defensively, it protected Harley-Davidson trademarks and helped clean up the marketplace by eliminating the vulgar t-shirts that flooded the market in the '70s.

The success of the turnaround continues. The 1993 Fortune survey of corporate reputations placed Harley-Davidson at the top of its industry (transportation equipment) for the third year in a row. A true High Performance Organization, Harley-Davidson ranks high among the "most admired" U.S. organizations.

THE GREENFIELD MODEL FOR THE HIGH PERFORMANCE ORGANIZATION

When using this high performance model to develop a new organization, the design and plan can focus on creating the *ideal* processes, systems, structures, and culture. There is no existing culture to change and no system to redesign. For a greenfield model, the generic steps are the same but the nature of the tasks are very different. For example, in the launch phase (Figure 8.6), one of the tasks is to "take necessary actions to *eliminate* redundancies." In a greenfield application the instruction "take necessary action to *eliminate* redundancies" would read "take necessary actions to *avoid* redundancies."

In a greenfield operation, the composition of the design teams and the definitions of their tasks will be completely different than those of an ongoing business. However, even in greenfield operations, creating a new-paradigm-based High Performance Organization requires attention to processes for handling change. Care must be taken in all start-up situations to ensure that a new paradigm culture emerges and not an old paradigm hybrid that must be changed once it commences operations.

IT ALL GOES BACK TO CULTURE

Even in a greenfield organization, newly hired people must undergo extensive cultural change. Change of this kind requires an interactive and simultaneous involvement of all five fundamental dimensions of culture: shared beliefs, values, and attitudes; communication systems; technologies; structure; and leadership.

The purpose of these high performance models is the same. They meet the needs of situations and circumstances under which change must be planned and implemented in all organizations. The models of change we have reviewed are designed to allow the leaders of organizations that must undergo change to select from the basic elements of culture those that best fit the needs. In every instance, the final result should be to produce an organization that is truly fast, focused, and flexible.

Conclusion

There is an ancient superstition of the sea that, inevitably, one wave comes along that is greater than any that has preceded it. It is called the Ninth Wave. It is the powerful culmination of sea and wind. There is no greater force. To catch the Ninth Wave at the critical moment requires a special skill, timing your movements to mount it at its peak.

Today we see such a powerful wave in our future. Our own Ninth Wave, bringing with it significant change. To catch this Wave, this change, we must prepare now. So that when it is our turn to respond, we can catch the mighty Ninth with the best that is in us and ride it all the way to the shore.[1]

THE BALL IS NOW IN YOUR COURT

You cannot decide whether we will fight or not. We will.
You can only decide one thing: Whether or not we shall be
victorious.

— Golda Meir

The purpose of this book is to help leaders make a difference. To accomplish this, it was necessary to write a book that is different from the modern genré, which takes one of two general formats. The first comes close to promising a miracle cure in the form of techniques. The second takes an "if they can, why can't you?" approach to explaining management fads and styles by using anecdotes.

Instead, I tried to answer four fundamental questions that are central to the creation and execution of strategies that can lead to prosperity and survival.

- ♦ What must be done?
- ♦ Why must it be done?
- ♦ How are the necessary strategic and organizational changes implemented?

♦ Why do people often have difficulty understanding the "whys, whats, and hows" central to an organization's successful transformation from the traditional management paradigm to the high performance paradigm?

In pursuit of these goals, a lot of ground was covered quickly. The structural transformation of the global economy produced market conditions that are best described by chaos theory. The result is Endemic Overcapacity, which was defined as follows:

Overcapacity simply means there is more supply than demand at price levels that permit acceptable operating margins.

Endemic, in this context, means that the threat of overcapacity faces every organization—if not today, then in the very near future.

The strategies that can successfully cope with Endemic Overcapacity are inconsistent with the cultures and structures of organizations based on the traditional paradigm. We explained what paradigms are—and what they are not—and investigated how an individual's knowledge structure affects his or her ability to recognize the need for change and to understand its implications.

To effect a paradigm shift, it is necessary to understand the following fundamental issues:

- What is the old paradigm?
- Why is it no longer adequate?
- What is the new paradigm and how does it differ from the old?

Shifting from one organizational paradigm to another is exponentially more difficult than shifting from one production technique to another, or from one marketing structure to another, or from one cost accounting system to another. Indeed, shifting from one organizational paradigm to another requires a significant cultural transformation.

We investigated organizational culture and its five interactive dimensions. The various models that can be used to guide the development and implementation of a plan to create a High Performance Organization are based on systematic approaches to changing the organization's culture.

The skill, will, and constancy of purpose of an organization's leadership must be combined with an organizational design and implementation plan to successfully transform an organization. Given the same plan and circumstances, some leaders perform better than others. Skill, technique, experience, practice, insight, and genius all have roles to play.

Most leaders who have successfully transformed an organization agree unanimously that however rapidly they forced change to occur, they should have moved even faster and more forcefully. The forces that inhibit change are strong. The slower the advance of the forces for change, the better the defense of the forces protecting the status quo.

The underlying causes of this phenomenon can be found in the Emotional Cycle of Change (Figure 9.1). The first four steps must be resolved quickly in order to get the associates into stages five and six. This involves *accepting change*, understanding its implications and urgency, and enabling associates to see *change as a source of hope* for the future. A quick review of these six stages should clarify why speed is central to success.

EMOTIONAL CYCLE OF CHANGE²

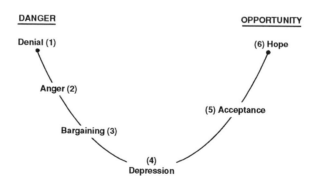

Adapted from Kubler-Ross *Model On Death and Dying*

Figure 9.1

Emotional Cycle of Change

1. **Denial and Isolation**
   a. Shock-gradual recuperation.
   b. Seeking support from different views.

2. **Anger**
   a. When denial cannot be maintained.
   b. Rage, envy, resentment.
   c. Why me?
   d. Goes in all directions, projected into environment.
   e. Plays out in numerous ways, with numerous people. Grievances, sabotage.
   f. If respected and understood, will calm down.
   g. We usually do not stop to consider a person's reasons for anger, only that we may be a target.
   h. Can stay in this stage – "I'll show them."

3. **Bargaining**
   a. Brief period.
   b. Consider other approaches to get what we want.
   c. Try to negotiate something different.

4. **Depression**
   a. Can no longer deny, no anger, cannot bargain away.
   b. Threat to self-esteem.
   c. Depression about the past and about the future.

5. **Acceptance**
   a. Dealt with (expressed previous feelings).
   b. Not to be confused with happiness – may be void of feelings.
   c. Peacefulness

6. **Hope**
   a. Previous stages represent defense mechanisms, coping mechanisms.
   b. There may be some possibilities – some opportunities – in all this happening.
   c. Person and institution (family or organization) get in tune with one another's needs.

Figure 9.1 (cont.)

189

When measurable improvements can be documented on dimensions critical to customers, organizational performance, and other stakeholders, efforts are producing the desired results. An example of an organization that is changing and improving is shown in the following arachnoid chart (Figure 9.2). The arachnoid is an excellent way to present key standards and measures in a compact display. Collective performance can be viewed in order to confirm that progress against one of the measures is not achieved at the expense of the other.

KEY STANDARDS AND MEASURES:
ARACHNOID EXAMPLE

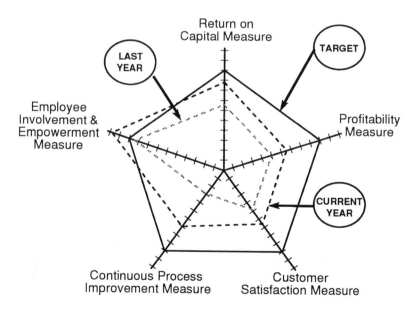

Figure 9.2

In this example, last year's performance is shown by the lighter dotted line, which can be compared against this year's performance as shown by the darker dotted line. The solid outer line represents the target. The standards and measures in this chart should help answer the question: "Is change occurring fast enough?"

An editorial in a leading business magazine discussed the progress of change in the auto industry. It gave insight into the tremendous upheaval required to continue to achieve competitive success, as well as the barriers to change encountered in large established bureaucracies.

"Both Ford and Chrysler are picking up market share in the U.S. because each in its own way has discovered how to build product-development teams that generate successful new models. Their method: Bring together people from engineering, design, purchasing, manufacturing, and marketing, and make them responsible as a group for the new car. Then destroy all bureaucracy above them, except for service support.

"GM has yet to do this. Its team members remain tied to their old structures—the engineers to engineering, purchasing agents to the purchasing department. Decisions aren't made for the good of the new product but to satisfy atavistic requirements of ancient bureaucracies.

191

"GM's new CEO, Jack Smith, is beginning to move against the auto giant's Byzantine bureaucracy, but he has a long way to go. He has cut corporate staff and accelerated the unification of GM's operating divisions into a single North American Operations structure. Smith knows the problems. The question is, can he move fast enough to solve them?"[3]

It is not enough to know what is needed. Fast, focused, and flexible systems based on knowledge are required. In the final analysis, success will depend on the quality of leadership. We have provided the bold new imperatives to form the foundation. It is up to you to provide the leadership.

A clear vision of the future is essential. The will and ability to act <u>swiftly</u>, <u>decisively</u>, and with <u>force</u> to achieve the organization's vision rests upon your shoulders as a leader.

The fate of your organization is in your hands. Can you see what the organization should become, and what its culture should be, for it to survive and prosper? Are you willing and able to do what it takes to transform it into a High Performance Organization? The ball is now truly in your court. If you are a leader, it is time to lead.

Rules for Leaders of High Performance Organizations

Attain consensus understanding of strategic objectives.

Determine key competitive advantages needed to achieve objectives.

Define core processes and systems—focus on those essential to goals.

Organize work around processes that add value.

Align structure and systems with vision and strategy.

Integrate suppliers and customers into *value chains.*

Eliminate departmental barriers—focus on the performance of business systems.

Create a hierarchy of processes and systems to replace the hierarchy of personal power.

Eliminate redundant layers of entrenched bureaucracy.

Streamline. Eliminate non-value-added work.

Set specific performance objectives for each process.

Empower employees.

Hold all accountable for their own performance.

Link training, appraisal, compensation, and budgets to customer satisfaction and organizational excellence.

Recognize that these rules do not produce a fad, but rather an organizational change of paradigmatic proportion!!

NOTES

Chapter 1: The Challenge of the New Economic World Order

1. Tichy, Noel and Stratford, Sherman. *Control Your Destiny or Someone Else Will.* New York: Doubleday, 1993.

2. Crichton, Michael. *Jurassic Park.* New York: Knopf, 1990.

3. Ibid.

4. Ibid.

5. Ibid.

Chapter 2: Knowledge Structures Keep Us From Hearing What is Being Said

1. Adapted from *Analogies at War.* Yuen Foong Khong, Princeton, NJ: Princeton University Press, 1992.

2. Ibid.

Chapter 3: The Evolution of the Traditional Management Paradigm

1. Johnson, H. Thomas. *Relevance Regained: From Top-down Control to Bottom-up Empowerment.* New York: The Free Press, 1992.

2. Jacques, Elliott. "In Praise of Hierarchy" *Harvard Business Review*. January-February, 1990. pp 127-133.

Chapter 4: Shifting Paradigms of Management

1. Parker, Wood (Lt. Commander). *Paradigms, Conventional Wisdom, and Naval Warfare*. Proceedings (US. Naval Institute). April, 1993.

2. Ibid.

3. Drucker, Peter F. *Management in Marketing*. New York: McGraw Hill, 1961.

4. Levitt, Theodore. "Marketing Myopia" *Harvard Business Review*. July-August, 1960. p 56.

5. Drucker, Peter F. *Management in Marketing*. New York: McGraw Hill, 1961.

6. Boyd, Harper W. and Massy, William F. *Marketing Management*. New York: Harcourt Brace Jovanovich, Inc., 1972.

7. Main, Jeremy. "Under the Spell of Quality Gurus" *Fortune*. August 18, 1986. pp 30-34.

8. National Productivity Review. *Strategic Quality Management: Turning the Spotlight on Strategic as Well as Tactical Issues*. Spring, 1994. pp 185-196.

9. Ibid.

10. Tetzeli, Rick. "Making Quality More Than A Fad" *Fortune*. May 18, 1992. pp 12-13.

Chapter 5: Changing Organizational Structure

1. Sun Tzu (500 BC). *The Art of War*. Oxford University Press, 1963.

2. Roget's II. Boston: Houghton Mifflin Co., 1988.

3. Horngren, Charles T. and Foster, George. Cost Accounting: A Managerial Emphasis. 6 ed. Prentice Hall Publishing, 1987.

4. Sun Tzu (500 BC). *The Art of War*. Oxford University Press, 1963.

Chapter 6: Introduction to the High Performance Organization

1. Seller, Patricia. "Companies That Serve You Best" *Fortune*. May 31, 1993. p 15.

Chapter 7: The High Performance Leader

1. Collins, James C. and Porras, Jerry I. "Organizational Vision and Visionary Organizations" *California Management Review Reprint Series*. The Regents of the University of California, 1991.

2. Ibid.

3. Stalk, G. "Time: The Next Source of Competitive Advantage" *Harvard Business Review*. July-August, 1988. p 44.

4. Dixon, Norman. *On the Psychology of Military Competence*. London: Johnathan Cape LTD, 1976.

5. Peter, Dr. Laurence J. *The Peter Principle*. William Morrow, 1969.

6. Patton, George S. *Patton: The War As I Knew It*. Boston, MA: Houghton Mifflin Co., 1947.

7. Petre, Peter (1992). *It Doesn't Take a Hero*. New York: Bantam Books, 1992. pp 200-201.

Conclusion: The Ball is Now in Your Court

1. *The Executive Speechwriter Newsletter*, Emerson Falls, St. Johnsbury, VT 05819.

2. Reprinted with the permission of Macmillan Publishing Company from *On Death and Dying* by Elisabeth Kubler-Ross. Copyright © 1969 by Elisabeth Kubler-Ross.

3. Kerwin, Kathleen with Treece, James B. and Woodruff, David. "Can Jack Smith Fix GM?" *Business Week*. November 1, 1993. pp 126-135.

INDEX